ROUTLEDGE LIBRARY EDITIONS:
MACROECONOMICS

Volume 4

MACROECONOMIC POLICY IN THEORY AND PRACTICE

MACROECONOMIC POLICY IN THEORY AND PRACTICE

JOHN BROOKS AND ROBERT W. EVANS

Routledge
Taylor & Francis Group
LONDON AND NEW YORK

First published in 1978 by George Allen & Unwin Ltd

This edition first published in 2016
by Routledge
2 Park Square, Milton Park, Abingdon, Oxon OX14 4RN

and by Routledge
711 Third Avenue, New York, NY 10017

Routledge is an imprint of the Taylor & Francis Group, an informa business

British Library Cataloguing in Publication Data
A catalogue record for this book is available from the British Library

ISBN: 978-1-138-93746-8 (Set)
ISBN: 978-1-315-67362-2 (Set) (ebk)
ISBN: 978-1-138-93889-2 (Volume 4) (hbk)

Macroeconomic Policy in Theory and Practice

JOHN BROOKS

and

ROBERT W. EVANS

London
GEORGE ALLEN & UNWIN
Boston Sydney

First published in 1978

GEORGE ALLEN & UNWIN LTD
40 Museum Street, London WC1A 1LU

British Library Cataloguing in Publication Data

Brooks, John
Macroeconomic policy in theory and practice.
– (Economics and society series; no. 6)
1. Economic policy 2. Macroeconomics
I. Title II. Evans, Robert W
339 HD82 78–40370

ISBN 0–04–339012–9
ISBN 0–04–339013–7 Pbk

Photoset in 10 on 11 point Times by
Northampton Phototypsetters Ltd
and printed in Great Britain
by Billing & Sons Ltd
Guildford, London and Worcester

Preface

This book is aimed at the student who has completed an introductory course in economics and who wishes to make use of and extend the economic theory taught in his introduction to economics in order to understand how such theory is applied in the conduct of macroeconomic policy. The application of the theory to the policy is illustrated with reference to postwar UK (and occasionally US) experience of conducting macroeconomic policy.

Chapter 1 introduces the idea of policy as a dichotomy between targets and instruments, briefly surveys UK macroeconomic policy since the war and discusses the meaning and desirability of the major objectives of macroeconomic policy. Chapters 2–6 examine the workings of the main policy instruments, with a discussion in Chapter 4 of the main theories of the term structure of interest rates and their respective implications for debt management as an effective instrument of policy. Chapter 7 is specifically concerned with the *simultaneous* achievement of the policy objectives, and to this end the main features of Tinbergen's 'fixed targets' and Theil's 'flexible targets' approaches to policy are outlined.

The book is directed towards two kinds of students. First, it is expected that students specialising in economics who are following second-year courses in macroeconomic theory will find the material here useful complementary reading. Secondly, it could be used by second-year students reading for other degrees in which economics is a major component but in which, due to time constraints, the relevance of theory to policy must be introduced at an early stage, e.g. other social science and business studies degrees.

Within a constraint of 70,000 words, some things have got to 'give'! We only hope that our choice of what to include and what to exclude is one that not too many people will disagree with.

Finally, we should like to thank Professor Colin Harbury, the series editor, who read earlier drafts and who made many helpful suggestions on how they might be improved.

JOHN BROOKS
Preston

ROBERT W. EVANS
Coventry

Contents

Chapter 1

Introduction to Macroeconomic Policy

Until relatively recently, the main role of government in economic affairs was that of fostering an environment in which the forces of the private market could operate to allocate resources among competing uses and to distribute the final product between the various factors involved in its production. That is, policy was concerned with the setting up and maintenance of laws and institutions that enabled market forces to operate more efficiently. Little consideration was given to the direct manipulation of such forces. Disappointment with the performance of most Western economies in the interwar years and the general acceptance of the ideas put forward in Keynes's General Theory led to a major reorientation of the role of Western governments in their conduct of economic affairs. This reorientation took the form of a more explicit economic policy, namely, an attempt to achieve simultaneously a number of generally accepted economic objectives. Evidence of this new approach is given by the increase in target consciousness since the Second World War. Governments have increasingly felt obliged to state target levels for employment, growth and inflation rates and balance-of-payments positions at which they should aim. Consequently, Kaldor (1971) states that 'governments have come to be judged by performance criteria which they would have strongly disclaimed in earlier days'.

MEANING OF MACROECONOMIC POLICY

Macroeconomic policy is concerned with how the agencies responsible for the conduct of policy can affect certain economic aggregates and in particular move them towards desired target levels, the achievement of which is deemed to increase national economic welfare. Shaw (1971) regards it as the 'normative counterpart of macroeconomic theory'. The latter attempts to formulate hypotheses to explain which factors are important in determining the level and changes in aggregates, whereas the authorities, in their exercise of policy, make use of those hypotheses which have been supported by empirical evidence.

Another distinction which is frequently made is that between macroeconomic policy on the one hand and microeconomic policy on the other. Going along with Shaw's terminology we might usefully think of microeconomic policy as the normative counterpart of microeconomic theory, which is concerned with the rational decision making of individual economic units, e.g. the decisions of individual consumers or firms. Consequently, explicit microeconomic policy can be regarded as action by the authorities that is intended to alter these individual decisions with the aim of affecting the allocation of resources. Examples of such policy are attempts to affect the output and pricing decisions of particular firms. The methods by which these changes can be brought about range from the imposition of specific taxes on particular producers through to legal sanctions and ultimately the taking over and running of some industries by the public sector.

The dividing line between the study of macroeconomic and microeconomic policy is more one of convenience than it is substantive. One cannot easily be divorced from the other. Many of the functional relationships between variables upon which macroeconomic policy is based have micro foundations, and actions taken at the macro level have microeconomic implications. The former is highlighted by a recent resurgence of interest in the microeconomic foundations of macroeconomic relationships, a good example of which has been the attempt to explain the relationship between aggregate consumption and income from a micro base. Similarly, examples of macro action having micro implications are many. One need only consider the differing impacts that various methods of raising or lowering the aggregate level of taxation will have. In order to raise aggregate taxation by a given amount there are a number of bases upon which the authorities may operate. If personal income is selected as the base, the raising of personal income tax rates may have the effect of causing certain individuals to reduce their supply of labour services; if taxes are levied on the sale of products of specific industries, this action will have a different set of micro implications, and so on.

So far we have seen that macroeconomic policy can be thought of as an attempt by the authorities to achieve particular target levels of certain major economic aggregates. Which techniques, however, are available to the authorities to enable them to bring such changes about? Here it is useful to extend our concept of policy to consider it in terms of the dichotomy between target variables and instrumental variables. The target variables are those which it is desired to set at particular levels, examples of which are the employment level, the inflation and growth rates and the balance-of-payments position. The first three are of interest because it is thought that the achievement of the desired levels of these adds fairly directly to national economic welfare, whereas the fourth is included more as a constraint on the achievement of the others rather than because it is anything desirable in itself. That is, a country benefits in real terms while running an external deficit, but as deficits cannot be financed indefinitely the achievement of external equilibrium sets a constraint upon the other objectives.

Instrumental variables can be thought of as those over which the authorities have fairly direct control in the sense that they can set the levels of these variables more or less accurately. Changes in the levels of the instrumental variables are then considered to affect the target variables through links, these links being the established models of macroeconomic theory. It is in this sense that the policy maker makes use of theory and empirical testing of the theory in his conduct of policy. Since a large proportion of this book is concerned with the instruments over which the authorities have control and the effect that changes in these instruments will have on target variables, it will suffice, in the remainder of this section, to briefly mention some practical and conceptual problems in the relationship between targets and instruments.

The first, a definitional problem, is what exactly is an instrumental variable? Can we give an example of one? To be precise, we shall think of two kinds of instrumental variables, and we shall refer to them as *primary* instrumental variables on the one hand and *intermediate* instrumental variables on the other. Primary instrumental variables are those which the authorities do have the ability to alter directly. As an example, in the field of fiscal policy, we can take tax rates. Taxes are levied upon a number of different bases, e.g. personal income, company profits and expenditures on particular goods. However, various rates can be applied to these bases in order to obtain a given tax yield from each base. Variation of these rates will consequently vary the revenue obtained from each base. In this example then the intermediate instrumental variable is the total tax revenue, and it is changes brought about in this that bring about changes in output and employment, the target variables. Therefore, in a sense there are two linkages: one between primary and intermediate instruments and one between intermediate instruments and targets. To make this important distinction clearer, let us consider another example, this time from the field of monetary policy. The manipulation by the authorities of the reserve ratios that commercial banks are obliged to observe is an example of the use of a primary instrument. The resulting change in the money supply, if indeed one does occur, represents a change in the corresponding intermediate instrument.

The above discussion on the linkages between the various types of variables leads us to a second, and more practical as opposed to definitional, problem. If the relationships between the different kinds of variables defined above were known exactly, such knowledge would greatly simplify the task of the policy maker. Unfortunately this is not the case; there is imperfect knowledge of the workings of the economic system, and consequently policy can only be conducted with an element of imprecision. One of the jobs of economists is therefore to try to understand these linkages more exactly if policy making itself is to improve.

Finally, the instruments of policy are sometimes classified into particular groupings, often according to which agencies are responsible for their use. However, such classification cannot be exact as there are a number of overlaps in these responsibilities. Furthermore, apart from the question of responsibility the instruments themselves will often not be independent. For example, action taken in the field of fiscal policy will frequently have implications for monetary policy. Bearing this in mind, however, we now mention a widely accepted classification of the instruments that are at the disposal of the authorities. Under monetary policy are included changes in the supply of money, interest rates, conditions of hire purchase and an instrument that was in vogue in the 1960s in the United Kingdom, namely, the various direct controls on the lending of commercial banks. Fiscal policy is taken to encompass changes in the composition and timing of the government's revenue from taxation and its expenditures. It is convenient to think of debt management policy as straddling both fiscal and monetary policies. This is so because the debt itself arises from the budget deficits of fiscal policy and because the way in which the debt is managed will have repercussions for the conduct of monetary policy.

Also included are a batch of instruments under the title of balance-of-payments policy. These are specifically manipulated in order to affect the country's external position, and they include the choice of exchange rate regime and the introduction of import quotas and tariffs.

Finally, we mention prices and incomes policies. These represent direct intervention in the workings of the market economy, and the increased use of such policies in the United Kingdom since the Second World War has been the result of increased demands on the authorities to achieve the objectives of macroeconomic policy simultaneously. Being under such an obligation has led those responsible for carrying out policy to look for new instruments to augment those already in their armoury.

OUTLINE OF UK MACROECONOMIC POLICY SINCE 1945

Following the disappointing economic performance of the interwar years and the acceptance of the ideas put forward by Keynes in his General Theory, UK policy makers, in common with many of those of other Western countries, emerged from the war with a strong commitment to a managed economy. At this time the main aim of this management was 'the maintenance of a high and stable level of employment after the war' (Cmnd 6527, 1944).

The year before the war ended saw the publication of two important documents which marked a turning point in the course of UK economic history. The first was the Beveridge Report, *Full Employment in a Free Society* (Beveridge, 1944). This radical document of its day laid down a policy that 'sets up a long-term programme of planned outlay by social priorities and designed to give stability and expansion to the economic system'. The main aspect of this policy was one of maintaining aggregate demand by a 'new type of Budget', in that government action should be concerned not only with adjusting its own outlay to movements in private sector investment but also with influencing directly both private sector investment and consumption. Specifically, the areas in which the government should intervene to maintain the planned outlay were given as a programme for the provision of such non-marketable goods and services as defence, education and a national health service and for the extension of public control in the running of industry, both by the nationalisation of certain industries and by the setting up of a National Investment Board which would aim to 'co-ordinate and steady the activities of businessmen'. Furthermore, it was proposed that private consumption, which formed a large proportion of total outlay, should be 'increased and steadied by State action in redistributing income, by measures of Social Security and by progressive taxation'. As already mentioned, these proposals were indeed radical in 1944, and they have led one writer (Winch, 1969) to suggest that the Report was a 'highly ambitious programme combining the aims of full employment with extensive social reform'. The spirit of the Report was Keynesian in that it was suggesting remedies to overcome the possible tendency for the postwar economy to move towards under-full employment equilibrium as had occurred after the previous war.

The scope of the remedies suggested by the Beveridge Report was wide, wider than that of the remedies contained in the second important publication of that year, namely, the government's *White Paper on Employment Policy* (Cmnd 6527, 1944). This represented the official commitment to postwar full employment, but its remedies were less adventurous than those of Beveridge. The main proposals in the White Paper were a programme of counter-cyclical public-investment planning and the variation of national insurance contributions to affect private consumption. It contained no proposals for directly affecting an important source of economic instability, namely, the fluctuations in private sector investment. Beveridge himself regarded the White Paper programme as much too conservative. He remarked that 'the policy of the White Paper is a public works policy, not a policy of full employment'. He was not convinced that its proposals were sufficient to maintain the aggregate outlay required to ensure full employment.

These then represented some of the main and most influential views as to which course the economy should take in the postwar years. The years immediately after the war were concerned with reconstruction and transition, and to this end many of the wartime economic controls were maintained. It was also a period of 'cheap money' which enabled inexpensive government borrowing at a time when the government was undertaking a large programme of nationalisation. Budgetary policy was used more and more to maintain a high level of overall demand, and consequently higher levels of employment were achieved than had existed before the war.

Unfortunately the apparent success of achieving high employment at this time began to lead to another difficulty which has plagued the UK economy since that time and which intensified after 1967. This was the problem of inflation. The requirement then became one of attempting to run the economy at a high level of activity while at the same time curbing the rate of inflation. To this end various experiments have been carried out since 1948 in the field of incomes policy (see Chapter 5). The first attempt at an incomes policy to overcome the trade-off between unemployment and inflation was that of the then Chancellor of the Exchequer, Sir Stafford Cripps. Cripps's efforts met with some success in restraining the rise in wages, but the policy eventually broke down because of price rises following the 1949 devaluation of sterling and the booming raw material prices during the Korean War.

While the main concerns of the immediate postwar years were reconstruction, social reform and the commitment to full employment, the 1950s witnessed increasing interest in a further objective of macroeconomic policy, namely, the rate of economic growth. Although Britain's postwar growth performance was an improvement on that of the interwar years, the desire for faster growth at this time was Britain's poor position *vis à vis* other western European countries. Consequently, the *White Paper on the Economic Implications of Full Employment* (Cmnd 9725, 1956) stated: 'The Government is pledged to foster conditions in which the nation can, if it so wills, realise its full potentialities for growth in terms of production and living standards.' Growth was not the only concern of this White Paper, and, as its title suggests, it underlined the concern about the problem of continually rising prices: 'one problem to which we have not yet found a satisfactory solution'.

Attempts at achieving the growth objective were constrained during the 1950s and 1960s by Britain's balance-of-payments problem. During these years Britain was operating a fixed exchange rate, and the recurring conflict between growth and balance-of-payments equilibrium came to be known as the stop–go problem. The 'go' referred to periods when the rate of growth of domestic demand, particularly private consumption demand, was increased through tax reductions and changes in credit control in an attempt to encourage business investment and through this, hopefully, the rate of economic growth. Unfortunately, with the fixed exchange rate regime the expansion of domestic demand quickly sucked in imports, bringing about a deterioration in the external position. Then in order to rectify this domestic demand was contracted (the 'stop' period), which resulted in increased unemployment and a slowing down in the rate of economic growth.

This policy of 'consumption-led' growth is one to which Kaldor, among others, has taken exception. He would have preferred that another component of final demand, namely, export demand, should have been the prime mover of an economy such as Britain's, i.e. an industrialised economy with a heavy involvement in international trade. In order to achieve this 'export-led' growth, Kaldor believes that, instead of maintaining the fixed exchange rate, the rate should have been 'managed' in the sense that it should have been adjusted in order to regulate foreign demand for UK exports, thus enabling this export demand to play the part of the prime mover of the economy. In his advocacy of such a policy, Kaldor (1971) lists what he regards as some of the main advantages that export-led growth has over the policy of consumption-led growth. One important weakness of the comsumption-led policy, in an economy operating a fixed exchange rate and in which export demand is insufficient to meet the growth potential, is that there is no provision for ensuring that resources can be transferred from consumption to investment. The reduction in private consumption releases resources for investment, but, since investment itself is dependent on the rate of growth of consumption demand, the incentive to invest is also reduced. With export-led growth, however, consumption can be reduced, and the managed growth in export demand will create the incentive to make use of the resources thus released to increase both export output and the capacity of the export industries. Under the fixed exchange rate regime, the UK authorities made a rate adjustment in 1967, namely, a sterling devaluation of 14·3 per cent, and eventually, in 1972, sterling was allowed to 'float' in order to remove the balance-of-payments constraint during a period when the authorities were making another 'dash for growth' (see below and Chapter 6).

A number of attempts at improving the policy towards growth were made in the 1960s. The first of these, namely, the setting up of the National Economic Development Council (NEDC), was conceived as a step towards French-style indicative planning. Its function was to examine future growth potential, to search out obstacles to growth and to seek agreement on ways to increase growth. To this end a number of Economic Development Committees were set up, each one concerned with the problems faced by particular industries in the achievement of their growth targets. With the advent of the Labour Government in 1964 some of the broader functions of the NEDC were shifted to the Department of Economic Affairs, which resulted in the publication of the National Plan in 1965. This was an attempt at longer term planning aimed at improving businessmen's expectations of future economic performance in the hope of encouraging increased investment and efficiency. However, further difficulties with the external position necessitated deflation to protect the fixed exchange rate, and actual performance fell below that projected by the National Plan.

Britain emerged from the 1960s with high rates of unemployment and inflation, compared with the average rates that had existed in the rest of the postwar period, with low growth but with a reasonably strong balance-of-payments position. Up to the mid-1960s there had been notable success in maintaining quite a low level of unemployment. Certainly it turned out to be much lower than the 3 per cent that had been taken as a rate acceptable to Beveridge. However, after 1966 unemployment became higher than anything experienced since 1945. A number of attempted explanations have been given for this recent increase in registered unemployment. Gujarati (1972) sees the explanation of this increase to be on the supply side of the labour market as the result of new social security legislation in the mid-1960s. The Redundancy Payments Act 1965 made provision for the payment of a lump sum to those made redundant, the size of the payment being determined by the length of time employed and the worker's average earnings. The National Insurance Act 1966 introduced a system of wage-related unemployment benefits. The suggestion is that those innovations enabled the unemployed to spend more time in search of employment and that in consequence a higher level of registered unemployment resulted.

Taylor (1972, 1974) believes that the main explanation is to be found on the demand side of the labour market. He contends that after 1966 there was a 'shake-out' of labour. Employers met the recovery of demand of 1967–8 by raising labour productivity rather than by employing new workers. Taylor believes that this change in the attitude of employers was the result of their pessimism about the United Kingdom's future prospects and that the switch from increasing men to simply increasing man-hours worked also owed something to the fact that overhead costs of employing labour had increased, due to the redundancy payments scheme and to levies payable to the industrial training boards.

The picture in the early 1970s was one of increasing unemployment, accelerating inflation, low growth but a reasonably strong balance-of-payments position. By 1971 unemployment had risen still further, and it was considered that some expansion should be undertaken. In order to remove the balance-of-payments constraint on its 'dash for growth' the Conservative government allowed sterling to 'float' in June 1972. Furthermore, in an attempt to contain the inflationary consequences of the expansionary policy a statutory incomes policy was introduced in late 1972.

Although there resulted a short term rise in output, the strategy failed to bring about the hoped-for breakthrough to faster longer-term growth. While the exchange rate depreciated there emerged a substantial deficit on the balance of payments, due mainly to a world commodity price rise which was occurring at that time and which culminated in the sharp rise in oil prices in late 1973 and 1974. In February 1974 one commentator was led to state: 'It is not often that a government finds itself confronted with the possibility of a simultaneous failure to achieve all four main policy objectives – of adequate economic growth, full employment, a satisfactory balance of payments and reasonably stable prices' (*National Institute Economic Review*, February 1974).

Since then a newly instituted voluntary incomes policy has been in operation, the government has taken steps to reduce the public sector's borrowing requirement (see Chapter 4), e.g. reductions in public expenditure, and sterling has depreciated further. Whereas unemployment has continued to rise and the rate of inflation has remained high, there have been favourable developments on the current account of the balance of payments, as the recession has depressed import demand and the falling exchange rate has caused some switch in demand towards UK-produced goods.

THE OBJECTIVES OF MACROECONOMIC POLICY

In this section we turn to an examination of some of the problems associated with the concepts of full employment, price stability, external equilibrium and a desired rate of economic growth. These are the generally accepted objectives of macroeconomic policy since a move towards the achievement of these targets is deemed to increase national economic welfare. This whole notion is fraught with difficulties, and we examine these in detail in Chapter 7. One problem is that more often than not all the objectives cannot be achieved simultaneously; a move towards one often results in a movement away from another. That is, trade-offs exist between some of the objectives, and as a result choices have to be made. With this very brief introduction to some of the problems associated with the theory of policy, we now turn to an examination of each objective in turn.

The employment objective

Full employment is a tricky concept to define. It certainly does not imply the employment of everyone of working age in the population. For one reason, there are always likely to be some people who, as a result of various disabilities, will find themselves unemployable. For another, at any particular time some workers will be in the course of changing jobs, during which period they will find themselves unemployed. That is not to say that policies should not be undertaken to reduce such frictional unemployment to a minimum. Also, since the achievement of high employment frequently conflicts with some of the other objectives of policy, the notion of full employment itself will be part of a choice problem in the sense that policy makers are only free to maximise employment subject to some price stability or balance-of-payments constraint.

Statistically, unemployment in the United Kingdom refers to the number of people (counted on one day of each month) who are registered at local employment exchanges and looking for work. As a result the figure of registered unemployment fails to indicate the total extent of unemployment. In particular it fails to include those who would be quite willing to work if work were available but who have no incentive to register as unemployed.

The incentives to register as unemployed are twofold, namely, to receive unemployment benefit and/or to receive help in obtaining alternative employment. In periods of economic recession the likelihood of swift re-employment will be slight, and if, coupled with this, there are individuals who are not entitled to unemployment benefit, their inclination will be to remain as unregistered unemployed and hence to leave the labour force. (The labour force is defined as those in employment, including the self-employed plus the registered unemployed.) Similarly, during an upturn in economic activity they may re-enter the labour force without having at any time registered as unemployed. This source of hidden unemployment means that the swings in the numbers of employed will be larger than those of registered unemployment. That is, in an upturn employment will increase by a larger amount than unemployment will fall, and in a downturn employment will fall by a larger amount than unemployment will rise. This bias in the statistics does not exist in US figures which are drawn up from sample surveys of households and hence 'capture' such hidden unemployment. As a consequence US unemployment percentages tend to be higher than their UK counterparts, and care must be taken in attempting any raw comparison.

Commonly, economists tend to distinguish three types of unemployment: demand-deficient unemployment, frictional unemployment and structural unemployment. The first category, as its name implies, is unemployment that exists because of an inadequate level of aggregate demand. It is sometimes referred to as Keynesian (or cyclical) unemployment since its removal can be achieved by an expansion of aggregate demand. Frictional unemployment exists due to the movement of labour from one job to another and is likely to be of short duration. It must therefore coexist with suitable vacancies that are within travelling distance and that are offered at prevailing wage rates. Finally, structural unemployment refers to much more serious mismatches in the labour market, namely, the existence of unfilled vacancies that the unemployed are unable to fill either because they do not possess the requisite skills or because vacancies are geographically too far removed from the unemployed to allow them to be taken up. Such mismatching can result from shifts in the relative supply of or demand for labour in particular regions or industries. For example, foreign competition in textiles and shipbuilding has over a long period caused a drop in the demand for the specific skills of those industries in the United Kingdom, whereas technological advance has increased the demand for computer programmers.

Each category of unemployment calls for a different remedy. Frictional unemployment may be reduced by systems that improve the dissemination of information about job opportunities. Structural unemployment across occupations may be lowered by retraining programmes, whereas geographical structural unemployment may be reduced by encouraging either firms or labour to be more mobile. As already mentioned, demand-deficient unemployment can be reduced by the expansion of demand.

Although it is not possible to fit any one unemployed person into any particular category of unemployment, with sufficient information on the characteristics of the unemployed and of the vacant jobs an attempt can be made to obtain some aggregate figures for these categories. Such an attempt has been made by Thirlwall (1974) following work in an earlier paper on these distinctions (Thirlwall, 1969). Using unemployment figures as a measure of labour supply and vacancies as a measure of labour demand (for an explanation of the difficulties of accepting these measures, see Thirlwall's papers), his classification is as follows:

$$U_T = U_F + U_S + U_{DD} \quad (1)$$
$$U_{DD} = U_T - V_T \quad (2)$$
$$U_S = V_T - V_R \quad (3)$$
$$U_F = V_T - V_W \quad (4)$$

where U_T is total unemployment, U_F is frictional unemployment, U_S is structural unemployment, U_{DD} is demand-deficient unemployment, V_T is total vacancies, V_R is vacancies of the right type and V_W is vacancies of the wrong type.

Equation 1 is clear enough. It says that total unemployment is the sum of the three categories discussed above. Equation 2 states that demand-deficient unemployment is the difference between total unemployment and total vacancies. Note that when total vacancies exceed total unemployment there is no demand-deficient unemployment, by definition; all unemployment is then either structural or frictional. Equation 3 states that structural unemployment is given by the difference between total vacancies and vacancies of the right type – right in the sense that there are some unemployed people who can take them up. Finally, equation 4 defines frictional unemployment as the difference between total vacancies and vacancies of the wrong type – wrong in the sense that none of the unemployed are qualified to take them up, because of either a skill or a geographical mismatch.

Most classifications involve difficulties. Thirlwall points out that this classification makes the measures of demand-deficient unemployment and non-demand-deficient unemployment, i.e. $(U_F + U_S)$, dependent upon the pressure of demand in the labour market. At a given pressure of demand U_{DD} is given by the difference between U_T and V_T. However, as demand expands, in an attempt to remove U_{DD} extra vacancies arise that are not suited to the characteristics of the unemployed, and consequently the non-demand-deficient component of unemployment increases. Also, the classification implies that structural unemployment will be the product of 'good' times rather than of 'bad' times. That is, in times of high levels of activity there are likely to be more vacancies for which the unemployed are unsuited, whereas in low activity periods fewer of these are likely to exist.

However, using this classification as a basis Thirlwall (1974) attempts to measure the types of unemployment in Britain in the period 1963–72. His first examination is on the assumption of complete geographical mobility, hence ruling out structural unemployment owing to a geographical mismatch. His main conclusion here is that over the period in question, which had an average level of unemployment of approximately half a million, one-fifth of these were unemployed due to skill mismatching. The average level of frictional unemployment over the period was 130,000. However, because of the mobility assumption this measure understates total structural unemployment, but when he measures the geographical aspect of structural unemployment he finds that this measure is much lower than that which results from occupational immobility. While he finds that on the whole geographical structural unemployment was low, it was higher for women than for men, indicating greater willingness among men to move between regions.

The objective of price stability

To most people it is clear why the maintenance of a high level of employment should be an objective of macroeconomic policy. The economic costs, in terms of output foregone, and the social costs, in terms of hardship caused, are obvious. However, it is not always as clear why another objective of policy should be a low inflation rate.

What is meant by inflation? Inflation may be described as a sustained rise in the *general level of prices* as measured by a price index. A price index is a weighted average of the prices of many goods and services in which the weight attached to the price of each good reflects the importance of that good in consumers' budgets. For example, in the calculation of an index of the general price level, the prices of housing and food which form a large proportion of consumers' expenditures will be given larger weights than the price of toothpaste.

Defining inflation as a sustained rise in the average price level means that inflation does not require that all prices should be rising in the same proportion or indeed that all prices should be rising; some might be remaining stable and some might even be falling. That is, during an inflation *relative* prices might be changing for a variety of reasons, e.g. good harvests for some crops, bad harvests for others and changing technology in the production of certain goods.

Although we have taken inflation to mean a sustained rise in the general level of prices as measured by a price index, there are a number of difficulties with this definition. The first concerns the adequacy of general prices indices as measures of inflation. As Johnson (1967) notes, they fail to 'take account of improvements in the quality of goods, nor do they do very well with introducing and incorporating the behaviour of the prices of new goods'. For example, if we were to compare merely the change in car prices between 1950 and 1977, our conclusion might be that they had risen substantially. However, much of the price increase may indicate an improvement in quality. Similarly, new products are usually not included in the construction of price indices until they have become standardised and established, ignoring the early period during which their prices are likely to have fallen.

Secondly, if certain goods are subsidised or taxed, should prices be taken net or gross of subsidies and taxes when an index of the general price level is being constructed? In spite of these difficulties we shall retain the notion of inflation as a sustained rise in prices as measured by a general price index.

Why should inflation be of concern? After all, what does it matter if we just add a few noughts to all our transactions? One reason put forward is that problems can arise in a situation where economic units, e.g. firms and households, find themselves unable to anticipate fully the future rate of inflation. This means that there will be an element of unanticipated inflation, which can lead to redistributions of real income and wealth that are thought to be socially unjust. How do such redistributions occur? As Bronfenbrenner and Holzman (1965) point out: 'Inflation alters the distribution of income and wealth because individual prices of current goods and services, productive factors, monetary and real assets and liabilities are not equally flexible and do not respond equally to general inflationary pressure.' For example, if wages rise less rapidly than prices in inflationary periods, labour will lose out as a result of inflation. Inflexibility of some prices may be the result of government action. For example, rent control can cause landlords to lose out, or the failure to compensate pensioners for inflation will militate against them. A second source of inflexibility may be the making of contractual agreements that have not made allowance for the actual future inflation rate. Creditors will lose out if they have contracted to lend money at interest rates that are insufficient to account fully for future inflation. Similarly affected will be the members of a trade union whose leaders have drawn up a long term contract that has not accounted fully for future inflation.

Apart from these redistributions, what are the truly economic costs of inflation? By economic is meant, are any resources misused or sacrificed because of inflation? In the face of inflation certain economic units might find it advantageous to invest some time and effort, through setting up research departments, to obtain a better idea of what the future inflation rate will be. Secondly, contracts might be drawn up more frequently between economic units requiring an additional use of resources. Even if inflation is anticipated fully there are economic costs. It is usually assumed that economic units wish, on grounds of convenience, to hold a certain amount of *real* money balances in order to carry out their transactions. By 'real' is meant a certain amount of nominal money divided by an appropriate price index. In other words, if the price level doubled, economic units would want to double their holdings of nominal money in order to keep their real holdings intact. That is, they want to hold a real amount of purchasing power. However, to the extent that money balances yield no pecuniary return the opportunity cost of holding them is the market rate of interest foregone. Now the advent of inflation that is correctly anticipated will cause the market rate of interest to increase more or less by the inflation rate. Hence the opportunity cost of holding money balances will increase, which will result in a decision by economic units to economise on their holdings of such balances. This is where the notion of an economic cost enters. Since the costs of producing money are negligible, whether it is in the form of notes and coins or as bank deposits, few resources are released by this economising on the holding of money balances. However, due to their decision to economise, economic units will be forced to employ more resources in moving more frequently between money and other financial assets. Similarly, economic units may incur costs in changing their payments procedures and habits, such as the costs of undertaking more frequent shopping expeditions and of storing goods that they have decided to hold rather than depreciating money.

One suggestion which is gaining popularity among some economists is the introduction of indexation into a wide range of economic relationships. That is, nominal contracts should be automatically adjusted for inflation, thus maintaining a real relationship. Therefore the nominal interest rate paid by debtors should rise to reflect the rate of inflation, labour market contracts should be altered to reflect the rate of inflation and government transfer payments should be adjusted likewise. Under the progressive income tax system, in which tax rates are set in nominal (not real) terms, inflation causes an increased share of a given amount of real income to be transferred to the government. Consequently it is also suggested that adjustments should be made to the tax system to offset this transfer resulting from inflation (see Chapter 2).

Among the claims made for indexation is that it would improve the allocation of resources by removing the need for individuals to anticipate inflation in order to make their economic decisions. For example, it is argued that due to an inability correctly to anticipate inflation (and consequently the real return from productive investment), certain investors may wish to purchase commodities whose values keep pace with the rise in the general price level, e.g. antiques, rather than to lend to those who will undertake productive investment. Another advantage, of course, would be the removal of the various redistributions mentioned above.

Balance-of-payments equilibrium

The attainment of a satisfactory external position has been an important objective in the United Kingdom since the war. In this section we briefly examine what is meant by the balance of payments and why the achievement of equilibrium can be regarded as a legitimate objective of economic policy.

A country's balance of payments (we take the United Kingdom as the country concerned) is defined as a systematic record of the economic transactions, during a given period, between its residents and those of the rest of the world. Conceptually, it is built up on the basis of double entry book-keeping. That is, every transaction has two sides, a debit and a credit, both of which are entered in the accounts. Any transaction that gives rise to a receipt from the rest of the world is recorded as a credit. The receipt itself can take many forms, e.g. a rise in UK residents' holdings of foreign assets or a decline in foreign liabilities, but whatever its form the receipt should be recorded as a debit. Conversely, any transaction giving rise to a payment to the rest of the world is recorded as a debit, but the payment itself, which also can take many forms, e.g. a reduction in UK residents' holdings of foreign assets or an increase in their liabilities to foreigners, should be recorded as a credit. Therefore imports are recorded as debits whereas payments for imports are recorded as credits; the reverse situation holds for exports. Similarly, if a UK resident makes an investment abroad the investment, since it implies a payment to foreigners, is recorded as a debit, and again the payment is recorded as a credit; the reverse situation holds for a foreign investment in the United Kingdom. Finally, if the UK authorities run down their holdings of gold and foreign exchange reserves, this is recorded as a credit in the accounts. It may appear strange that the sale of foreign exchange holdings is a credit. Well, it follows from above: any transaction that creates a demand for the domestic currency (sterling), e.g. exports and foreign investment in the United Kingdom, is recorded as a credit; therefore the running down of foreign exchange reserves in order to absorb any excess supply of sterling is recorded as a credit.

We have only been able to remark on a few transactions, but the following questions arise. If each transaction is entered in the accounts twice, once as a credit and once as a debit, must not the balance of payments always balance? What then is meant by a deficit on the balance of payments? The answer to the first question is that yes, the accounts must always balance the way we have presented them. Before examining the second question we shall briefly look at another way in which the balance of payments may be classified. Transactions can be classified according to their nature, and two broad classifications are commonly mentioned, namely, transactions that enter the *current account* and those which enter the *capital account*. The current account includes those transactions which directly affect the country's national income, i.e. transactions that create or use national income. The current account can be subdivided into the *balance of visible trade*, which is concerned with the flows of exports and imports, and the *invisible balance*, which consists of items such as banking and insurance services, tourism, expenditure by the government on military services abroad, profit and interest payments on investments abroad (minus profit and interest payments to foreigners who have made investments in the United Kingdom) and private transfers.

Broadly speaking, the capital account includes inflows and outflows of long-term real (direct) and portfolio investments, short-term capital movements and the borrowing and lending that is undertaken between the UK government and other governments. Real investments, e.g. UK firms setting up plants abroad, are undertaken because of higher expected profits by operating abroad; portfolio investments, e.g. purchases of foreign securities by UK residents, are undertaken because of a higher expectation of return than if domestic securities were purchased. Short-term capital movements are made to take advantage of interest rate differentials between international financial centres. Finally, the capital account also includes transactions affecting the country's reserve position, e.g. changes in the country's holdings of gold and foreign currency reserves.

We saw above that, since the accounts are conceptually drawn up under the principle of double entry book-keeping, the total of credits must equal that of debits. It follows then that the balance on the current account should always equal the negative of that on the capital account. For example, a current account deficit must be matched by a surplus on capital account. This result is analogous to that of an individual's economic transactions over a period. Suppose that, over a period, an individual's expenditure exceeds his income. This excess must have its counterpart in the individual's 'capital' account. He can either use up past savings (run down his reserves), borrow from other units or liquidate some of his assets in order to accommodate his excess expenditure. He may of course select some combination of these three possibilities.

But the balance of payments still balances. What is meant then by a balance-of-payments deficit or surplus? As Cooper (1966) states: 'Defining surplus or deficit . . . entails some systematic exclusion of certain credits or debits from a set of accounts which must "balance" when taken as a whole.' Therefore certain entries are segregated from the other entries in order to define deficits or surpluses. A whole literature has grown up around the justification of any such segregation. We shall take the balance-of-payments concept proposed by the Berstein Committee (1965). This definition, known as the 'official settlements balance', enters in the measure of deficits or surpluses only a few selected items, namely, the transactions of the official financial authorities of the country concerned. That is, in the measure of deficits or surpluses are entered (1) changes in the country's reserves and (2) changes in its liabilities with the International Monetary Fund (IMF) and other foreign official monetary institutions. The justification of this definition of imbalance is that it measures the degree of pressure exerted upon the authorities that is caused by the country's international transactions. During periods of deficits the problem is that the country's reserves are decumulating and/or that it is accumulating debts to either the IMF or other foreign monetary authorities; during surplus periods the reverse is occurring.

The pressures imposed upon the authorities in deficit periods and those imposed in surplus periods are asymmetrical. The former are more immediate than the latter. Since any country's reserves must be finite and since foreign monetary authorities are likely to become increasingly reluctant to lend as borrowings become greater, the elimination of a deficit can be regarded as a legitimate objective of policy. Less obvious, however, is why the removal of a surplus might be an objective. After all, accumulating reserves or other claims on foreigners might be regarded as an acceptable thing to do. However, here the concept of opportunity cost comes to our aid. Let us take an extreme case but one that illustrates the point. Imagine that a particular country undertakes no foreign investment and that foreigners have no investments in the country under consideration. Further imagine that the country exports some goods but imports nothing. It is then running a balance-of-payments surplus and accumulating foreign reserves. The opportunity cost of this surplus is the amount of goods that the country is sending abroad and that it could be consuming itself.

So far we have been implying that the objective for external equilibrium should be to eliminate any tendency towards a balance-of-payments surplus or deficit, i.e. to achieve a zero change in reserves (forgetting claims on or of foreign monetary authorities). This, however, begs the question: why have reserves in the first place? Reserves give a country breathing space and help it to avoid making painful adjustments in the face of a change in external circumstances (an emergence of a deficit) that is only temporary. For example, if the country were unwilling to allow its exchange rate to depreciate at all (or to depreciate sufficiently to remove the deficit), then in the absence of adequate reserves one policy option would be the contraction of domestic demand and subsequent increase in the level of unemployment. Therefore the correct objective should perhaps be, not to achieve a zero balance, but to ensure that, on average, over a reasonable length of time, the level of reserves remains such as to provide sufficient liquidity to mitigate the need for painful internal adjustment.

The objective of economic growth

Until relatively recently there was widespread agreement between economists, laymen and politicians on the need to improve the growth performance of the United Kingdom. The work of Mishan (1969, 1977) and others has shown up some of the costs of growth and produced serious reservations about the desirability of increasing the growth rate in Western developed economies. In spite of these reservations, which are mentioned below, growth still ranks high on the list of policy objectives.

Growth is commonly thought of as the expansion of productive capacity. It should be distinguished from short term fluctuations in the utilisation of existing capacity, which to a large extent tend to be demand induced. For example, in moving from a situation of high unemployment towards full employment by a policy of demand expansion, the short term growth of output can be much higher than the long term growth trend. In 1972–3 the United Kingdom achieved a growth in output of approximately 5 per cent, but this was not sustainable for long. Although we are emphasising the distinction between capacity growth and the utilisation of existing capacity, this is not to say that the two are independent of each other. First, during a period in which the utilisation of existing capacity is being increased it is likely that some of the increased output will itself contribute to an expansion of capacity. Similarly, prolonged periods of unemployment are likely to adversely affect the long run trend of capacity growth.

However, the essentials of the growth issue are best seen when we realise that economic growth is concerned with society's balance between present and future consumption. Growth is concerned with a sacrifice of present consumption which must occur so that resources can be directed to uses that allow a higher future level of consumption than would otherwise be possible. That is, resources can be used either to satisfy current consumption or to expand future productive possibilities. This expansion of future production, brought about by investment in physical and human capital, allows a higher future level of consumption than would occur in its absence. Therefore, if in a fully employed economy it is desired to raise future consumption, resources must be made available to bring this about, and this implies a sacrifice of current consumption. In an economy with unemployed resources, however, both current and future consumption levels can be raised. This is a problem of the underuse of existing capacity and as such is not the growth issue. The distinction between consumption and investment, where the latter is regarded as a future output raiser, is not always clearcut. In less advanced countries current food consumption will, by improving the physical wellbeing of the population, have some output-raising features.

When growth is looked at in this light it is clear that maximum growth is unlikely to be a desirable objective. Maximum growth in this sense would require the sacrifice of all but a barest minimum of current consumption. Such an approach to the distribution of consumption over time is not likely to be an acceptable state of affairs. What will be desirable, however, is a distribution of consumption over the present and future that in some way maximises society's welfare. This brings us to the correct objective, namely, the achievement of *optimum growth*, not maximum growth. This concept of optimum growth is simply defined by Beckerman (1974) as 'that growth rate at which the sacrifice of present consumption (or welfare defined as widely as one likes) in order to obtain faster growth is just offset by the extra future consumption that this faster growth will permit'. The concept involves two distinct sets of interest rates. The first, commonly referred to as society's *time preference* set, measures society's marginal rate of substitution as between consumption now and consumption at various dates in the future. That is, it is concerned with how much extra consumption in five, ten or twenty years in the future is worth the sacrifice of a given amount of consumption now. This is a subjective set, and as such economists, as economists, can make no judgements. However, optimum growth also involves another set of interest rates, commonly referred to as the *technological* set. This answers the question: how much extra consumption can be obtained five, ten or twenty years hence if the sacrifice is made of a given amount of current consumption? This is non-subjective; it depends on present and prospective technology.

These notions can be made clearer if we restrict ourselves, for purposes of illustration, to the choice of consumption levels in only two time periods, as illustrated in Figure 1.1. Present consumption is measured on the horizontal axis, and consumption in the future period is measured on the vertical axis. Curve *AB* represents the technological possibilities for substituting future for present consumption, and the indifference map represents society's valuation of future as against present consumption. It is clear that welfare is maximised at point *D*. At this optimum the rate at which society is happy to substitute future for present consumption, which is

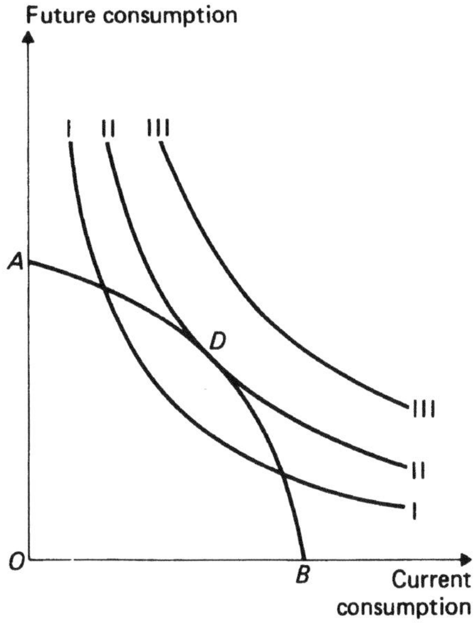

Figure 1.1 *Choice between present and future consumption*

reflected in the slope of the indifference curve II, is equal to the rate at which society can substitute future for present consumption, which is reflected in the slope of curve *AB*.

The consideration of the growth issue in terms of the choice between present and future consumption levels necessarily involves what is called *intergenerational equity*. That is, the concern is not only with the individuals who are alive today balancing their own consumption between now and the future, but also with the individuals who are alive today balancing the amount they are to consume against the amount they shall bequeath to future generations. Therefore the notion of future consumption, as we have used it above, must be widened to include the consumption of unborn generations.

It is unlikely that the optimum discussed above is ever attained, and consequently much debate surrounds what the attitude of the authorities should be towards growth. Those who have favoured government policies to encourage faster growth have emphasised certain imperfections that tend to militate against future consumption. For example, certain investments yield benefits over and above those captured by the private individuals undertaking them. An example is where an investment takes the form of resources devoted to research and development. Where such spillover benefits do exist there may be underinvestment from a social point of view.

Another argument for raising the growth rate is that individuals have insufficient consideration for the interests of their descendants.

This is expressed in what is known as the isolation paradox. That is, individuals would be willing to bequeath more to future generations if they believed that other individuals would do the same. However, since the market mechanism cannot bring about such an arrangement it has to be achieved through collective action, i.e. the political process.

Growth as a prime objective of policy has not gone unchallenged. Mishan's attack on it is concerned with what he sees as a number of external diseconomies that have accompanied the growth process, namely, increased pollution, noise, etc. He contends that it is incorrect to conclude that economic growth necessarily entails the expansion of an individual's area of choice and, even if the area of choice is expanded, that this results in increased welfare. His argument regarding the first contention is that we can regard a situation as being one in which choice has expanded only if in that situation goods that were previously available remain so. With growth this has not been the case; goods previously available are no longer so, and in addition certain 'bads' like pollution and aircraft noise have been introduced. Secondly, in so far as a man's welfare is dependent not upon his real income in an absolute sense but upon his relative position in the income scale, a given increase in real income affecting everyone equally will not result in a welfare increase. This is the *relative income* hypothesis.

CONFLICTS BETWEEN OBJECTIVES

Earlier when we sketched an outline of postwar policy in the United Kingdom we frequently mentioned how certain objectives of policy came into conflict. The major conflicts considered were those of growth and employment conflicting with external equilibrium and the conflict between employment and price stability. Such conflicts constituted a major reason for the difficulty in conducting a totally successful policy, in the sense of achieving the objectives simultaneously. In Chapter 7 we shall examine some of the main conceptual problems associated with the simultaneous achievement of the policy objectives, and in particular we shall look at two approaches to this problem: one associated with Jan Tinbergen and the other associated with another Dutch economist, Henri Theil. However, now we turn our attention to a closer examination of some of the main instruments used in attempts to achieve policy objectives.

Chapter 2

Fiscal Policy

In the introductory chapter a brief mention was made of the fact that the instruments of policy can be conveniently classified under the headings of fiscal policy, monetary policy, balance-of-payments policy, and prices and incomes policy. With this chapter on fiscal policy we begin a close examination of these various instruments. Our concern will be with how the authorities' manipulation of instruments attempts to achieve the main objectives of policy. However, with the inflation and balance-of-payments objectives we reserve separate chapters for a fuller discussion of these. One reason for this is that, in the case of inflation, we require discussion of some possible explanations of the inflationary process before examining the part played by demand management policies and prices and incomes policies in its curtailment. Similarly, with regard to the balance of payments, we require a certain amount of groundwork relating to the foreign exchange market before we can make a satisfactory assessment of how instruments may affect the external objective.

DISCRETIONARY AND AUTOMATIC BUDGET CHANGES

Essentially, by fiscal policy we refer to discretionary changes in the level, composition and timing of government expenditures and revenues from taxation. Along with private investment expenditure and expenditure on exports, government expenditure constitutes an injection into the circular flow of income; with private sector saving and expenditure on imports, taxation constitutes a withdrawal from this circular flow.

Consequently, discretionary changes in the government's budget position, i.e. the difference between expenditures and revenue from taxation, will in general tend to bring about changes in the level of economic activity. That is, a discretionary change that increases (decreases) the size of the government's budget deficit (surplus) is likely to be expansionary whereas one that increases (decreases) the budget surplus (deficit) is likely to be contractionary. (For a qualification of this which is related to the differing impacts of equal changes in government expenditures and taxation revenues, see below.)

Although a change in the budget position can result from action by the authorities to bring such a change about, the budget position may change automatically as the level of economic activity itself changes. That is, the budget position may change in the absence of discretionary actions by the authorities. This occurs since in most fiscal systems the levels of government expenditures and taxation revenues are not fixed but vary as the level of national income itself varies. For example, a large proportion of the total of the UK government's tax receipts comes from the taxes levied on personal incomes and on the profits of companies. As these two tax bases vary with the level of national income, so does the government's revenue from taxation. Similarly, certain government expenditures, e.g. payments to the unemployed, also vary with the level of economic activity. What the authorities set are levels and structures of rates, but, given these, the government's budget position becomes endogenous to the economic system, depending, as already mentioned, on the level of economic activity.

Therefore an observed change in the deficit or surplus may be the result either of a government decision to change tax rates and/or its expenditures or of a changing level of national income which has been brought about by, for example, a change in private sector investment through the multiplier. Failure to recognise this distinction between discretionary and induced changes in the budget can, for example, lead to the observation of an actual budget change that indicates a restrictive fiscal policy whereas the authorities' policy has in fact been an expansionary one. This situation is illustrated in Figure 2.1. The schedule T_0 relates the level of tax revenues at each level of gross national product (GNP). T_0 represents a given system of tax rates. That is, for a lower set of rates this schedule would be lower. It indicates that tax revenues rise as GNP

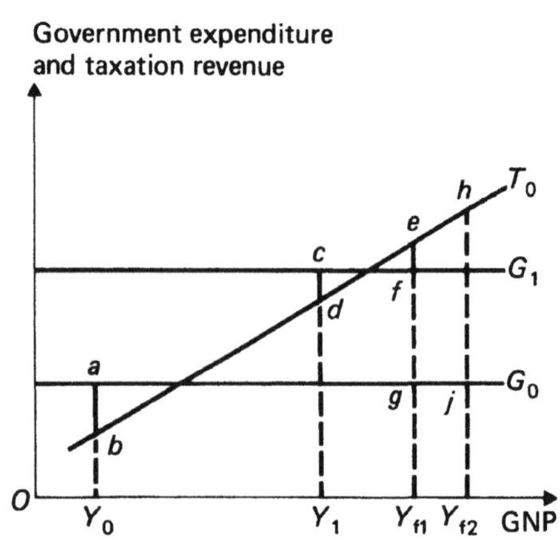

Figure 2.1 *Automatic and discretionary budget changes*

rises, and its slope indicates the response in tax revenues to a change in GNP. This is referred to as the built-in flexibility of the tax system; the steeper is the T_0 schedule, the greater is the degree of built-in flexibility.

The schedule G_0 represents the initial level of government expenditure. For simplicity it is assumed that the level of this expenditure does not vary as GNP varies. Earlier it was mentioned that some government expenditures would vary with income, but dropping this does not detract from the main argument.

Assume that with an initial level of expenditure of G_0 and a tax system represented by T_0, the level of GNP is Y_0. Consequently the budget is in deficit at Y_0 by an amount *ab*. Suppose, however, that the government decides that its expenditures should be increased to G_1, keeping tax rates and hence schedule T_0 as before. Further imagine that the increase in expenditures causes GNP, via the multiplier, to rise to the level Y_1. At this level the budget deficit is equal to *cd*, which is smaller than the initial deficit *ab*. Hence, making the crude observation that the actual budget deficit has diminished may lead to the mistaken conclusion that policy has been restrictive. As we know, however, the policy was in fact an expansionary one, increasing GNP from Y_0 to Y_1. This misconception arises because of a two-way line of causation: not only does a change in the budget affect activity, but in addition a changing level of activity affects the budget. What is required, therefore, is a method for separating these two effects. One such method, popularised in the early 1960s in the United States, is to examine what the budget position would be at a full-employment level of income, i.e. to examine the *full-employment budget surplus*.

In Figure 2.1 then, before the increased government expenditures took place, the budget position at the full-employment level of income, Y_{f1}, is given as a surplus equal to *eg*. When expenditures have increased to G_1 the full-employment surplus is reduced to *ef*, indicating an expansionary policy which was in fact the case. It should be noted that, in this case, an examination of the change in the budget associated with any level of income would have indicated the correct discretionary policy undertaken.

PROBLEMS WITH THE FULL-EMPLOYMENT BUDGET SURPLUS

Although a change in the full-employment budget surplus is an appealingly simple concept as an indicator of the direction and strength of fiscal policy, it carries with it a number of difficulties. One major practical problem is the estimation of the level of income that would be associated with full employment and of the tax revenues and government expenditures that would then apply.

Apart from this measurement problem there are, associated with the use of the full-employment budget surplus concept, some problems of a more conceptual nature. Earlier, reference was made to the fact that a discretionary change that increased (decreased) the budget deficit (surplus) was an expansionary one and vice versa. However, changes in government expenditures have a greater impact on economic activity than changes in taxation revenue of the same amount. This results from the fact that changes in expenditures affect activity directly whereas taxation changes only do so indirectly by affecting consumption expenditures. More precisely, an increase of, say, £1,000 m. in government expenditures will have a more powerful effect on activity than a reduction in taxation revenues of £1,000 m., because in the latter case part of the increased disposable income resulting from the tax reduction will be saved by consumers and consequently less than the £1,000 m. will be passed on to increase aggregate demand in the economy.

This important consideration is relevant to the use of changes in the full-employment budget surplus as an indicator of the strength and direction of discretionary fiscal policy. Since changes in government expenditures give 'more bangs per buck' (to use the inelegant American textbook phrase) than do changes in taxation revenues, an accurate assessment of the effect of a budget change requires a knowledge of how the budget change is composed, e.g. whether the change was totally composed of an expenditure change, totally composed of a taxation change or composed of some combination of both. As an extreme example, consider the case of an equal increase in government expenditure and taxation revenue. Since the expansionary impact of the increase in expenditure is greater than the contractionary effect of the change in taxation, the overall effect is expansionary. However, because the expenditure and taxation changes are equal, no change in the full-employment budget surplus will have registered, thereby giving the impression that no discretionary policy has taken place.

Another problem with the full-employment surplus arises in the context of a growing economy. The concept, it will be remembered, is an attempt to distinguish automatic from discretionary budget changes. However, in a growing economy the level of income associated with full employment increases period by period, and therefore, with unchanged government expenditures and tax rates, the full-employment budget surplus increases over time. Such an increase does not signify a discretionary contractionary policy; it is an automatic change which has been termed by Walter Heller (1966) as 'fiscal drag'. Later we shall see that inflation, as well as real growth, also gives rise to 'fiscal drag', since tax rates tend to be set in nominal terms. Heller's notion of drag is illustrated in Figure 2.1. Suppose that, in a particular period, full-employment income is given by Y_{f1}, with expenditure at the level G_0 and the tax schedule represented by T_0. The full-employment surplus is then *eg*. After real growth, full-employment income rises to Y_{f2}, and consequently the full-employment surplus rises to *hj*. Unless discretionary adjustments are made in tax rates and/or government expenditure, 'this automatic rise in revenue will become a "fiscal drag" siphoning off too much of the economic substance out of the private economy and thereby choking expansion' (Heller, 1966).

A more serious blow is levelled at the usefulness of the concept when it is realised that, as a result of a fundamental change in the tax structure, the direction of movement of the full-employment surplus may be totally opposite to the movement of the actual surplus. Blinder and Solow (1974) illustrate this point, and it is explained in Figure 2.2. Let the level of expenditure be G_0 and the original tax system be represented by T_0 with the actual level of GNP at Y_0. The actual budget position is a deficit of *ab*, with a full-employment surplus of *cd*. Now, however, a change in tax policy takes place which causes the new tax schedule to be T_1. The actual budget change is an increased deficit to *eb*, whereas the full-employment surplus has increased to *gd*. In other words, the change in the full-employment surplus has indicated contraction although the actual impact of the policy change has been an expansionary one at the current level of GNP. For this reason, Blinder and Solow suggest the use of changes in the *standardised surplus* as a measure of discretionary policy. That is, instead of using full-employment income as the point of reference, they suggest the use of current GNP as the reference point.

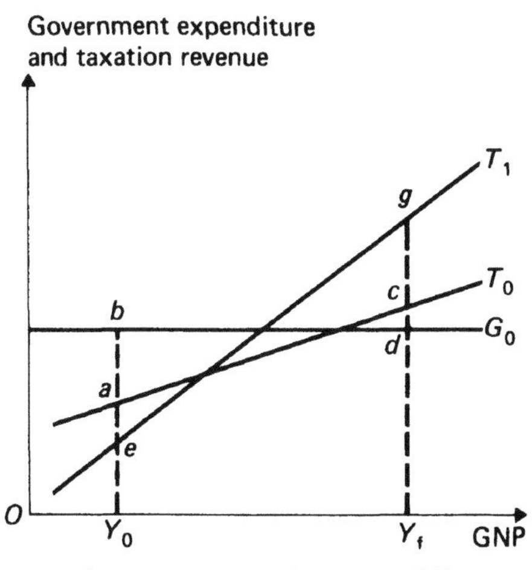

Figure 2.2 *A change in the tax structure that has a different impact on the actual budget surplus than on the full-employment surplus*

Smyth (1970) points out two further problems associated with the use of the full-employment surplus as an indication of policy changes: one is the use of the concept in a dynamic context, and the other concerns the place of the price level in measuring the size of the actual and full-employment surpluses. Although Heller's 'fiscal drag' is a dynamic problem facing the full-employment budget surplus concept, Smyth is concerned with lags associated with changes in government expenditures and taxation. Whereas changes in expenditures affect GNP fairly directly, changes in taxation revenue may affect it after a fairly long time lag, due to a possible delay in the response of consumption expenditures to changes in disposable income. If this is the case, then 'the time path followed by income will differ according to whether changes in full-employment budget surpluses are brought about by changes in government expenditures or by changes in taxation'.

Since price level changes are unlikely to be the same at all levels of GNP, which price level should be used to value budget deficits and surpluses? If the current price level is used to measure the actual budget position, should this also be used to measure the full-employment surplus? If it is, a different value will be obtained for the full-employment budget surplus, depending on the actual level of GNP. This is so since the price level is different for each level of GNP. Alternatively, should the level of prices that would exist at full employment be used to measure surpluses and deficits at all levels of activity? Here again a fundamental problem arises because, if all actual deficits and surpluses are to be measured at constant full-employment prices, some of the tax system's built-in flexibility will be overlooked because tax rates are set in nominal, not real, terms; consequently, a rise in real income that is unaccompanied by a price level change will result in a smaller increase in tax revenue than a rise in real income that is accompanied by a price rise. In terms of Figure 2.1, if T_0 is drawn on the basis of constant prices it will be less steeply sloped than if price changes are taken into account. In a final comment on the usefulness of the full-employment budget surplus concept, Smyth states that 'it is unlikely that the complexities of fiscal policy and its related effects on the economy could be expressed in terms of a simple one-dimensional measure'.

FISCAL POLICY AND THE STABILISATION OF ECONOMIC ACTIVITY

With the exception of a brief mention of fiscal drag and of the difficulties faced by the full-employment surplus concept because of the different periods of time that it may take government expenditure and taxation changes to affect the level of activity, most of the discussion in the last section was couched in static terms. However, some of the main problems in conducting policy are the result of policy being conducted in a dynamic setting. Because of the existence of lags and the inaccuracy of much economic forecasting, many economists are of the opinion that discretionary stabilisation of the UK economy has been unsuccessful and may have even aggravated fluctuations that already existed. With regard to monetary policy, this has led Friedman and others to advocate the simple rule of a steady growth in the money supply at a rate commensurate with the real growth of the economy and the abandoning of any attempts at discretionary policy. In this section some aspects of the use of fiscal policy for stabilisation are examined, including the comparison of discretionary policy with the use of so-called automatic stabilisers. Finally, some evidence about British postwar attempts at stabilisation are looked at.

Perhaps the main case against dependence on discretionary fiscal policy (and monetary policy) is the existence of lags in the economic system and the still unsatisfactory state of economic forecasting. While some of these lags are associated with the behavioural relationships, e.g. the time taken for consumption expenditure to react to changes in disposable incomes as a result of a tax change, others are the result of institutional arrangements and as such are likely to differ from country to country. Examples of such lags are, first, the time taken for the collection and processing of statistical information so that an accurate picture of the state of the economy can be obtained and, secondly, the time taken for political decisions to be made and for legislative action to be carried out. Inevitably the latter depends upon the constitutional arrangements of the country concerned. Musgrave and Musgrave (1968), as American observers, marvel 'at the speed with which so major a change as the Selective Employment Tax was enacted, with what seemed to be a minimum of explanation and discussion! In the United States, a two-year period would have been required to launch and legislate such a change.' A further feature of the British system which reduces the legislative lag is the so-called 'regulator' whereby the Chancellor of the Exchequer can vary indirect tax rates by up to 10 per cent (of the present rate) without requiring parliamentary approval.

Lags that occur before any policy action is undertaken are commonly referred to as 'inside lags'. Once the policy action has been carried out there exists another set of lags, 'outside lags', which are concerned with the time taken for the policy change to affect the ultimate variables to be controlled. For example, once consumer spending has been affected, say by a tax reduction, firms do not automatically increase their employment of labour until they are fairly certain that the resulting increase in demand is not merely a transitory phenomenon. Obviously, the longer are these lags, the longer will be the time taken for the policy action to affect the ultimate objective and the greater will be the likelihood of the action aggravating the fluctuations in activity. That is, if an expansionary policy does not take effect until the economy is being pulled out of a recession by other forces, the resulting boom could possibly be greater than that which would have existed in the absence of the policy. Similar considerations apply to a contractionary policy that does not bite until well after a downturn.

As a result of these problems and the difficulties that they pose for the conduct of policy, interest has been taken in what are commonly known as built-in or automatic stabilisers. These stabilisers are features of the economic system that act to reduce the multiplying effect on national income of changes in any of the components of aggregate demand. We have already come across one such feature in the previous section, namely, that in most tax systems the revenue from taxation varies with the level of GNP. On the expenditure side, there is the feature that unemployment compensation payments increase in periods of economic downturns, thereby cushioning the fall in disposable income that would occur due to the increased unemployment.

Before examining the operation of automatic stabilisers in a static context, it is worth mentioning that D. J. Smyth has shown that under certain conditions, in a dynamic context, the built-in flexibility of taxation revenues may lead to instability rather than have a stabilising impact. Smyth (1963) has demonstrated that this is possible in a model in which consumption is a lagged function of disposable income and in which investment expenditure depends on changes in income, lagged one period. More recently he has thrown up the same possibility in a model in which taxation revenues are dependent on lagged income (Smyth 1975). In this case the instability of the built-in flexibility of taxation can occur even when consumption expenditure is allowed to depend on income without any lag. The moral is therefore that care must be taken in interpreting any analysis of built-in stability where it is carried out purely in static terms.

With the use of a simple model of income determination, it is easy to demonstrate the automatic stabilising that is characteristic of the taxation side of the budget when tax revenues vary with income. The simple general model is given by the following system of equations:

$$Y = C + I + G \tag{1}$$
$$C = a + b(Y - T) \tag{2}$$
$$T = tY \tag{3}$$

where Y is national income, C is consumption expenditure which is dependent upon disposable income, $(Y-T)$, and taxation, T, is a function of income, with t representing the marginal tax rate. It will be useful to examine the size of the multiplier in three circumstances: in the total absence of taxation, under a lump sum tax and where taxation is dependent upon income. Without taxation the multiplier is given by $1/(1-b)$. Under lump sum taxation the consumption function is given by

$$C = a + b(Y - T) = (a - bT) + bY$$

In other words, as shown in Figure 2.3, the lump sum tax has the effect of shifting the consumption function (drawn against national income, Y) downwards by the amount bT. The important point, however, is that the value of the multiplier is unaffected, and consequently lump sum taxation makes no contribution towards built-in flexibility.

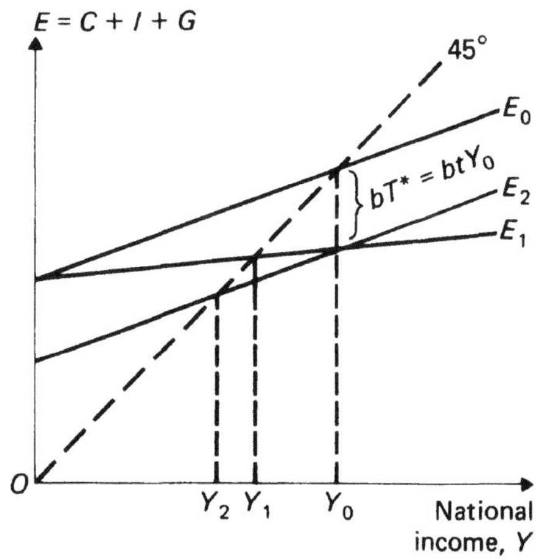

Figure 2.3 *The effects of lump sum taxation and income dependent taxation on the aggregate expenditure function*

When we now allow taxation to depend upon the level of national income, as represented by equation 3 above, the consumption function becomes

$$C = a + b(Y - tY) = a + b(1 - t)Y$$

Now the marginal propensity to consume national income becomes $b(1-t)$, and consequently the multiplier is given as $1/[1-b(1-t)]$. Since the marginal tax rate is less than one, $b(1-t)$ will be less than b, and therefore the multiplier with taxation as a function of income will be less than the multiplier without, with the result that income will be changed by a lesser amount if one or other of the components of aggregate demand is changed.

The lowering of the multiplier when income-dependent tax revenues are introduced is illustrated in Figure 2.3. For simplicity only total expenditure functions are shown, but since government expenditure and private investment are assumed to be independent of the income level, the effect that taxation has on the consumption function will be the same as its effect on total expenditure. Let E_0 represent the total expenditure function before any taxation system is introduced. Therefore the equilibrium level of income is the level Y_0. We now compare the effects of two kinds of taxation: a lump sum tax of an amount T^* and an income-related tax levied at such a rate that the revenue that it yields, *at the original level of income*, is equal to that of the lump sum tax. This allows an easy comparison of their respective effects.

The lump sum tax shifts the total expenditure function E_0 to the position E_2 – a vertical shift of bT^*. As a result the equilibrium level of income falls all the way to Y_2. The income-related tax has the effect of swivelling the E_0 function to E_1 with the equilibrium level of income falling only to Y_1. The smaller income change in the latter case is because, as income falls, taxation revenue falls accordingly, reducing withdrawals from the circular flow of income.

There are a number of features that make for a successful built-in stabiliser. First, the yield (in the case of a tax) or payout (in the case of expenditure) should be flexible with respect to changes in national income. Such flexibility is the result of two factors: the flexibility of the tax base with respect to income and the flexibility of the rate structure. Therefore the built-in flexibility of a proportional tax depends upon the responsiveness of the tax base to changes in GNP. In the case of a progressive tax a further factor adds to built-in flexibility, namely, the responsiveness of the *average* tax rate (the ratio of the tax yield to the base) to changes in the size of the base. That is, if the elasticity of the tax base with respect to GNP is greater than one and/or the elasticity of the average tax rate with respect to the base is greater than one, then the tax yield will change more than in proportion to the change in GNP. As a simple example, progressiveness of the income tax system is the result of rising marginal rates. Consider the case of an individual whose income in a particular period is £1,000. His tax allowances are £500, leaving taxable income of £500. The tax schedule is as follows: the first £400 of taxable income is taxed at 20 per cent, the second £400 at 30 per cent and the third £400 at 40 per cent. His total tax bill is therefore £110, i.e. an average tax rate of 11 per cent. Now suppose that in the following period his income rises to £1,500. With unchanged allowances and marginal rates his tax bill rises to £280, giving an average tax rate of 18·7 per cent. Another way of expressing this is that, while income has risen by 50 per cent, tax payments have risen by 154 per cent. On the expenditure side of the budget, the introduction of earnings-related unemployment benefit in 1966 added rate flexibility to this particular built-in stabiliser.

Secondly, and fairly obviously, an efficient built-in stabiliser must be such that the base is a large component of national income. For example, a highly progressive tax on peanuts is unlikely to play a major part in automatic stabilisation.

Musgrave and Miller (1948) suggest a simple measure of the effectiveness of built-in flexibility, namely,

$$B = 1 - \frac{\Delta Y_b}{\Delta Y}$$

where ΔY is the change in income in a system without built-in flexibility and ΔY_b is the income change with built-in flexibility. This measure indicates the fraction of the income change that is prevented by the presence of built-in flexibility. If $\Delta Y_b = 3$ and $\Delta Y = 4$, the fraction of the income change that is prevented is one-quarter. It is not likely that built-in flexibility can hold income entirely steady, i.e. make B equal unity, because it cannot overcome the original movement in income. For example, if the original change resulted from a given change in private investment expenditure, built-in stability can at best eliminate the multiplier effect of this change; it cannot reverse the original change in investment. That is, at best we should expect the income change to be limited to the change in investment.

Smyth (1966) criticises the use of such static measures and alternatively suggests as a suitable measure 'the extent by which the standard deviation of income is reduced by the introduction of built-in flexibility of taxation'. His suggested measure is then

$$B = 1 - \frac{\mathrm{SD}(Y')}{\mathrm{SD}(Y)}$$

where SD(Y) is the standard deviation of income without built-in flexibility and SD(Y') is that of income with it.

It was mentioned above that it would be unrealistic to expect built-in flexibility to be successful in completely stabilising movements in income, with the implication that some discretionary action might be called for. This leads to the problem, however, that those features which make for built-in stability by lowering the multiplier value also weaken any given impact of discretionary changes. A further argument that weakens the case for too much dependence upon built-in stabilisers is that there is no reason to suppose that their stabilising influence will be at a high level rather than at a low level of economic activity. For examples of studies that attempt to assess the automatic stabilising impact of certain taxes and expenditures, see Pearse (1962) for the former and Thirlwall (1969a) for the latter.

THE EFFECT OF INDEXING FOR INFLATION ON STABILISATION

In the earlier section on discretionary and automatic budget changes we came across Heller's concept of fiscal drag whereby, as a result of real growth and in the absence of discretionary changes in government expenditures or in the parameters of the tax system, there is a tendency for the fiscal surplus (deficit) to increase (decrease) over time. In that section, it was also mentioned that inflation also gives rise to 'drag' since tax rates tend to be fixed in nominal (not real) terms. In this section we look at this more closely and, in particular, at a way in which it might be corrected and what the implication of such correction would be for the built-in stability of the income tax system.

Because of the high inflation rates that many Western countries have experienced in recent years, an increased interest has been taken in the possibility of indexing various aspects of the economic system. As an illustration, our present concern is with the indexation of certain income tax parameters. Allen and Savage (1975) have made an estimate of the impact of inflation on the UK income tax system and found that it worsened the real income positions of those at the extremes of the income scale.

The combination of inflation and a progressive income tax system, in which the rates are set in nominal terms, affects tax liabilities in a number of ways. First, inflation reduces the real value of personal allowances, which increases the proportion of a given level of real income that is liable to taxation. Inflation also reduces the real threshold points at which the various tax rates become operative, and finally any resulting increase in money income may push taxpayers into higher tax brackets. As a result, inflation transfers command over resources from the private sector to the public sector if no discretionary offsetting changes are made.

Earlier we used an example of an individual taxpayer to show how, as his income rose, so did his average tax rate. We assumed an increase in income of 50 per cent, but at that time we did not specify whether his income increase was all in real terms, merely the result of a 50 per cent inflation or the result of some real increase and some increase due to inflation. For the purpose of our present discussion, let us suppose that the increase from £1,000 to £1,500 was merely the result of a rate of inflation of 50 per cent. In this case his real income is left unchanged, but he is now paying a greater proportion of it in taxation.

In order to prevent this purely inflationary aspect of fiscal drag, some method of indexing the parameters of the tax system could be introduced. Perhaps the simplest method would be to raise allowances and the starting points of the tax brackets by an index of the inflation rate, e.g. changes in the retail price index, while leaving the marginal tax rates unchanged. With our individual, when his income was £1,000 he was paying 11 per cent of his income in tax. We now assume that as a result of a 50 per cent inflation rate his income rises to £1,500. If we make the suggested changes in the tax parameters his allowances now become £750, leaving a taxable income of £750. Raising the threshold points by the inflation rate, the first £600 is taxed at 20 per cent and the remaining £150 at 30 per cent. This makes his total tax liability £165 and leaves his average tax rate unchanged at 11 per cent. We have chosen the extreme case of the income change being purely the result of inflation. However, more than likely some of the increase would have been a real increase, and the indexation exercise would not have removed all of the drag.

It should be obvious by now that the indexation of these taxation parameters would weaken the built-in stability of the taxation system by removing that element of it which is due to inflation. Indeed this was one fear of the 1966 Canadian Royal Commission on Taxation, which stated: 'To develop a tax system that taxed only income in "real" purchasing power would irreparably damage the built-in stability of the system.' In spite of such reservations, the Canadian government instituted such a scheme in 1974.

EVIDENCE OF UK POSTWAR STABILISATION POLICY

Assessment of the success or otherwise of economic policies is a difficult business. In the first place, there is an attempt to compare what actually did occur with a 'what might have been' situation, and the latter is something about which it is extremely difficult to be certain. Secondly, often there is an attempt to discover the success in achieving one particular objective of policy, and to this end the behaviour of the other target variables is often neglected. Consequently, care must be taken in interpreting the mass of empirical work that has been carried out into how successful postwar UK fiscal policy has been in stabilising the level of economic activity. For example, Matthews (1971) states that 'stabilisation of the level of activity was not as such the objective. For most of the postwar period, a better summary description of the objective would be the achievement of as high a level of activity as was compatible with the state of the balance of payments.' Along the same lines, Artis (1972) says that 'most of the time it was not the government's aim to stabilise. Its concern was with the balance of payments under the guise of "defending the parity" or of "making devaluation work".'

With these reservations in mind, however, we look briefly at the methods and conclusions of some attempts to throw light on this stabilisation issue. Broadly speaking, there are two approaches to making this kind of assessment. The simpler one is to attempt to discover whether or not the policy response, in the sense of changing one or other of the fiscal policy instruments, has been the 'correct' one for a particular change in the target variable. For example, taking the level of unemployment as the target variable, the question to be answered is: when there was a rise in unemployment, were the changes made in the instrumental variables the 'correct' ones to counteract the original movement in unemployment?

Such an approach has been used by Prest (1968) and Musgrave and Musgrave (1968). In Prest's case the only instrument considered is government expenditure. He correlates the percentage deviations of government expenditure from its trend with a measure of the percentage of unused resources, where the latter gives an indication of the level of economic activity. The resulting correlation coefficient is found to be −0·603. That is, during periods of low activity (high percentage of unused resources) government expenditure tended to be below its trend, and conversely. Although Prest admits that 'no simple deduction about the perverse influence of government spending policy on the cycles in the last few years can be drawn from this picture', he does say that the negative sign of the correlation coefficient hardly indicates a stabilising pattern.

The more detailed study undertaken by the Musgraves relates the responses of fiscal instruments on both sides of the budget, i.e. both expenditure and taxation changes, to changes in a number of target variables which include the growth rate, the unemployment rate and the balance-of-payments position. Their conclusion is also that policy changes cannot be said to have been stabilising. In particular, they state that 'the policy requirements imposed by the various goals moved in diverse and frequently conflicting ways'. For a detailed criticism of the methods of these studies see Worswick (1970).

The second approach is to use the 'what would have occurred' method and then compare this with what actually did happen. Bristow (1968) attempts a study along these lines – a study that is confined to the taxation side of the budget. Using estimates of the effects of various taxes from an earlier study, he removes the impact of taxation for the years 1955–65 and compares this result with what actually happened. He concludes that 'not only did the tax changes made during the period stimulate national income but they also had a stabilising effect' – a conclusion that most other studies do not come to.

While Bristow deals with only the taxation side of the budget, Hansen (1969), in a study which covers seven countries of the Organisation for Economic Co-operation and Development (OECD), attempts to assess the impact of the whole budget. Again with the use of estimates of the multipliers for various kinds of budget changes, he subtracts the effect of the budget from the actual behaviour of GNP to give a 'pure' cycle of GNP. He is then in a position to assess the stabilising effect of the budget on activity by comparing the behaviour of the 'pure' cycle with the behaviour of the actual cycle around the trend of actual GNP. Using this technique he concludes that UK policy was destabilising, whereas US policy achieved a substantially higher degree of stabilisation than that of any of the other six countries in the study.

A strikingly different result is thrown up if an extra dimension is added to the problem. Snyder, one of Hansen's co-workers, adds such a dimension for three of the countries in the Hansen study, namely, the United Kingdom, the United States and Sweden. Snyder (1970) measures the effects of budget changes in relation to potential (full-employment) GNP. Over time, the growth of potential GNP depends upon the growth of the labour force and the growth of productivity. As in the Hansen study, the total impact of budget changes are subtracted from the actual behaviour of GNP to give the 'pure' cycle, i.e. how GNP would have behaved in the absence of fiscal policy. The gap between the pure cycle and potential GNP is defined as *potential stabilisation*. In other words, policy is regarded as stabilising if it decreases this gap and destabilising if it increases it. The level of actual GNP in any one year indicates whether or not policy was stabilising in this respect. For the period 1955–65, Snyder concludes that the United Kingdom achieved 27 per cent of this potential stabilisation with the corresponding figures of 17 and 64 per cent for the United States and Sweden respectively. Hence Hansen's result for the United States must be qualified in the sense that it must be realised that the US achievement was to stabilise around the trend of actual GNP but at a level of activity well below potential.

One final point must be mentioned with regard to the 'what would have occurred' method of assessing policy. The pure cycle is not pure in the sense that it incorporates the effects of monetary policy changes, and the estimates of potential GNP are themselves dependent upon economic policies that affect the growth of the labour force and of productivity.

Chapter 3

Monetary Policy

MONETARY POLICY AND ECONOMIC ACTIVITY

Monetary policy can be regarded as affecting aggregate expenditure in that it causes disequilibrium to arise in the balance sheets of economic units, i.e. firms, households and financial intermediaries, and as affecting economic activity in that these units attempt to restore equilibrium in their balance sheets.

A balance sheet is simply a statement of an economic unit's assets, liabilities and net worth at a particular moment in time. The accounting convention that the balance sheet must always balance is ensured by the fact that net worth is defined simply as the difference between assets and liabilities. With regard to their balance sheets, economic units face two major kinds of decisions. First, for any given size of balance sheet, i.e. total of assets and liabilities, what should be the composition of assets and liabilities? Secondly, should the size of the balance sheet be altered? For example, should a unit borrow, i.e. incur a liability, to enable it to hold more assets? In order to examine balance sheet decisions in somewhat more detail, it is useful to classify economic units into two general categories, namely, those in the non-financial private sector (households and firms), and financial institutions.

To begin with it should be noted that all assets – whether they be money, financial assets, consumer durables or physical capital – can be conceived of as giving an interest yield (return) to their holder. The use of the term 'interest' here may confuse those who are used primarily to applying the term to the pecuniary return from financial assets, but, conceptually, a rate of interest is simply a way of relating the *flow* of services from an asset to the *price* of that asset. For example, consider the case of an infinitely long-lived motor car whose market price is £1,000 and which yields services each year worth £100 to its owner. We may then say that the interest yield (rate of return) of this motor car asset is 10 per cent. Therefore the notion of the return from assets is a wide one. We have just seen how the return from a 'motor car asset' is conceived of in terms of the services provided by the car. Similarly, the return from holding money consists of the services that money provides, e.g. convenience and security.

The fundamental principle governing decisions about the composition of the balance sheet is that the rate of return on marginal units of each asset (including money and other assets whose returns are in terms of the services they provide) must be equalised. Consider the consequences if this condition were not met. The economic unit would then transfer part of its resources from assets with the lower return to those with a higher return, and this process would continue until, at the margin, the returns on each asset were equalised. A similar principle would determine the size of the unit's balance sheet. That is, the unit would be willing to borrow (incur a liability) until the cost of the additional borrowing was equal to the return on the assets that the additional borrowing was being used to purchase.

All financial intermediaries (banks and non-bank intermediaries, e.g. building societies and insurance companies) can be thought of as behaving in the same way. Intermediaries issue their liabilities to lenders in exchange for surplus funds which lenders are holding. For example, banks and building societies offer their deposits and insurance companies offer policies in exchange for the surplus funds of lenders. (Note that certain of the liabilities of banks, i.e. current account liabilities, which are transferable for the settlement of debts and convertible into cash on demand, are included in what is known as the M_1 definition of the money stock along with notes and coins in circulation. Wider definitions of the money stock include the deposit account liabilities of banks.)

With the funds deposited with them, financial intermediaries purchase earning assets; banks hold a wide variety of assets, ranging from short-term financial assets to maintain their liquidity position to advances to customers, building societies lend to house purchasers against mortgage, and insurance companies are large holders of both government and company securities. The determination of the total of assets and liabilities of any group of financial intermediaries can be thought of as following the general pattern outlined above. That is, assets are held until marginal yields are equalised, and the size of the balance sheet is such that the additional cost of issuing liabilities (borrowing) is equal to the return from holding additional assets.

The determination of the total of assets and liabilities of a group of intermediaries is illustrated in Figure 3.1. Schedule MC_F (the marginal cost of attracting funds) indicates that additional funds can only be attracted at increasing cost to the intermediaries. These costs comprise two parts. The first part consists of any pecuniary return paid to the holders of the intermediaries' liabilities; for example, building societies pay interest to their deposit holders. The second part consists of any non-pecuniary services provided

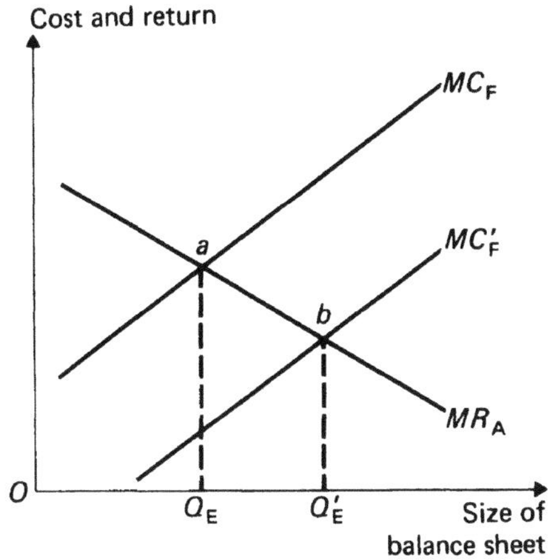

Figure 3.1 *Determination of equilibrium balance sheet size*

to the holders of the liabilities; for example, the commercial banks operate a payments mechanism for economic units holding their current account liabilities. Additionally, the intermediaries may have to incur more advertising costs in order to borrow more funds.

Schedule MR_A indicates that the intermediaries will only be able to acquire additional earning assets by lowering the yield they are prepared to accept; that is, the marginal return declines as the size of the intermediaries' business expands. The increasing marginal costs of attracting funds and the declining marginal yield of earning assets produce an equilibrium for the size of the balance sheet, namely, at Q_E in Figure 3.1, beyond which point the additional return from purchasing an earning asset is insufficient to cover the additional cost of attracting the funds to finance the purchase of the asset.

With the above framework established we now turn to an analysis of the effects of some of the primary instruments of monetary policy on economic activity. We concentrate our attention on two instruments, namely, open market operations and reserve requirements.

Open market operations

An open market operation is one where the monetary authorities enter financial markets either as buyer or sellers of government securities, offering or demanding cash in exchange, for the purpose of altering the supply of money in the economy. Let us restrict our attention to the case where the authorities purchase securities, i.e. an expansionary open-market operation.

The initial effect of the authorities' purchase of securities will be to push up their prices and lower their rates of return. The reason for this is straightforward. It is reasonable to assume that the return from holding money balances – a return which, as mentioned above, is in terms of the convenience and security that money holding affords – declines as more and more money balances are held. Therefore, as the authorities are giving economic units money in exchange for securities, these extra money balances will yield diminishing marginal returns to their holders. But since the return on assets must be equalised, the return from holding government securities must fall (in order to induce economic units to surrender them in exchange for money), and this comes about from a rise in their prices. However, this cannot be the end of the story, because so far nothing has been mentioned about what has happened to the returns on other assets, either other financial assets or physical assets which economic units may hold. The return on marginal money balances will now be below that on these alternative assets, and consequently, at the ruling set of relative returns, economic units will be holding money balances in excess of the amount they desire to hold. Therefore economic units will rearrange their holdings of assets to regain equilibrium; that is, they will substitute out of their excess money holdings into such assets.

One possible line of substitution for the excess holdings of money balances may be to use them to purchase the liabilities of a wide range of financial institutions. However, whichever particular group of intermediaries is involved, the general principle is the same. As economic units substitute the liabilities of financial intermediaries for money, the intermediaries are able to place their liabilities with holders at less cost to themselves. This process is illustrated in Figure 3.1, where the marginal cost schedule shifts to MC'_F, and the equilibrium for this group of intermediaries moves from point *a* to point *b* with the quantity of liabilities issued rising from Q_E to Q'_E. This increase in liabilities implies a concomitant increase in assets held by the financial intermediaries. These extra assets will be diverse and will depend on the particular group of intermediaries concerned. While the assets may be diverse, they will have one common characteristic in that they allow economic units to make expenditures that increase aggregate demand in the economy.

Besides the liabilities of financial intermediaries, there are other assets to which holders of excess money balances may turn, e.g. bonds, equities, consumer durables, direct purchases of physical capital and investment in 'human' capital (education and training).

If economic units that have surplus money balances attempt to substitute bonds for their excess money balances, bond prices rise (interest rates fall), making the financing of investment by bond issues cheaper. Consequently, economic activity is stimulated through the multiplier effect of increased investment.

Equities (shares) are claims of part ownership of companies' assets and are issued by firms to enable them to obtain control over physical capital. When economic units that have surplus money balances purchase equities, forcing up their prices (and lowering their yields), the value of the firms' capital will rise above the supply price of new such capital. Firms are then induced to increase their demand for more capital equipment, raising output and employment in the capital goods industries, with a consequent multiplier effect throughout the rest of the economy. The extent of the increase in output of the capital goods industries will depend on capacity constraints in these industries and on the existence of unutilised assets which can be brought back into operation. This channel of operation of monetary policy is emphasised by neo-Keynesians, e.g. Tobin (1963).

A similar argument (to that of equities above) applies to consumer durables, especially if second-hand markets exist for such assets. If the holders of surplus money balances use them in an attempt to purchase existing consumer durables, e.g. second-hand cars, the prices of second-hand consumer durables are raised relative to the prices of newly produced consumer durables. This leads to an increase in demand for newly produced consumer durables, raising output, income and employment in the industries producing these goods.

So far we have given examples of some of the assets that may be substituted for money when economic units find themselves holding surplus money balances and of how such substitutions will affect the level of economic activity. The assets purchased by economic units that hold surplus balances will be those which the units regard as being most closely substitutable for money, and this is an empirical matter. Those economists referred to as 'neo-Keynesians' contend that financial assets are those which are the closest substitutes for money and that, consequently, increases in the supply of money will have their effect eventually on the level of economic activity by bringing about increases in the output of the capital goods industries.

On the other hand, another school of economists, namely, the 'monetarists', contend that there is no one particular group of assets that is more closely substitutable for money than any other group and that, consequently, excess money balances will be used to purchase a wide variety of assets, e.g. financial assets, physical assets, consumer durables, and so on. Therefore the associated range of expenditures triggered off by an increase in the supply of money is correspondingly varied. The monetarists argue that the effect on any one expenditure category may well be quantitatively small but that the total effect is a pervasive increase in aggregate demand. For a now classic discussion of monetarist and neo-Keynesian positions and of the mass of empirical evidence that has been produced in an attempt to resolve the issues between them, see the Bank of England (1970).

Reserve requirements

The essential nature of legal reserve requirements is that they impose a constraint on the assets that financial intermediaries, particularly banks, are allowed to hold. The intermediaries are required to hold a minimum proportion of their assets in certain prescribed forms. The most important feature of those assets which count as reserves is that they have a lower return than most of the other assets held by the intermediaries. The reason for this is twofold: first, the assets involved are usually very short-term liquid assets; secondly, by making the intermediaries demand such assets, demand for them is artificially stimulated, thus forcing up their prices and lowering the return on them.

Therefore the major effect of an increase in reserve requirements for a group of financial institutions will be to lower the revenue obtained from any given volume of intermediation, i.e. a total of assets, by artificially forcing the institutions to hold lower yielding assets. The introduction of a reserve ratio, or an increase in the reserve ratio (if one already exists), will result in a reduction in the amount of intermediation conducted through these institutions, and this in turn will involve a fall in the level of spending in the economy. The rationale for the cut in spending is straightforward. If the intermediaries are now making less return on their assets, due to the reserve requirements, they can but offer less return on their liabilities; consequently, holders of idle balances will see less inducement to channel these balances through the intermediaries to potential spenders. The imposition of reserve requirements is analogous to the imposition of a tax on the intermediaries. There have been other controls on the amounts of certain assets that financial institutions may hold, e.g. the curbs on bank advances in the United Kingdom during the 1960s, but these will be discussed below.

Whatever the actual method of monetary control, the basic causal sequence is the same. That is, monetary policy affects aggregate demand in the economy by throwing the balance sheets of economic units out of equilibrium. Aggregate demand is affected as units seek to restore equilibrium.

MONETARY POLICY AND ECONOMIC GROWTH

Useful for our purpose is a simple model of the growth process. This is given as

$$\dot{Q} = \dot{A} + E_k \cdot \dot{K} + E_l \cdot \dot{L}$$

This suggests that the growth rate of output, $\dot{Q}$, is equal to the growth rate of technical progress, $\dot{A}$, plus the growth rate of capital, $\dot{K}$, times the elasticity of output with respect to capital, E_k, plus the growth rate of labour, $\dot{L}$, times the elasticity of output with respect to labour, E_l. However, the effect of investment on growth in such a model is likely to be underestimated. For example, Solow (1959) has developed a model that makes the rate of growth of technical progress a function of the rate of growth of the capital stock, the assumption being that new machines are more efficient than old ones. Therefore an increase in investment will reduce the average age of the capital stock, thus increasing the rate of technical progress. Whether or not one accepts this argument, it is clear that great importance is attached to investment as an 'engine of growth'.

Monetary policy has conventionally been thought of as an effective instrument for altering the rate of investment in physical capital by industry. What is the rationale for this belief? Suppose the authorities undertake an open market purchase of their securities. As argued above, economic units will find themselves in possession of excess money balances and will attempt to substitute the excess balances for other assets. The nature of such substitution is a major factor in the issue under consideration.

Above we saw that one group of economists, the neo-Keynesians, tend to limit the potential range of substitution to a narrow range of financial assets, with the result that the main thrust of monetary policy on aggregate demand is seen as occurring through the demand for new capital equipment. It was also mentioned above that monetarists see the substitution out of money as taking place along the whole spectrum of assets, with a consequent impact on a wide range of expenditures.

Whichever of these two schools of thought is nearer to the truth will have a profound influence on the effectiveness of monetary policy for promoting growth. The simple model at the beginning stressed the role of capital accumulation. We have seen that neo-Keynesians stress that the initial impact of monetary policy is on capital investment, while monetarists, although not totally neglecting this possibility, regard it as only one of many affected expenditures, any one of which is possibly of a small magnitude.

UK MONETARY POLICY AND ALLOCATIVE EFFICIENCY

It is safe to say that during the 1960s in the United Kingdom the major aim of domestic monetary policy was the control of aggregate demand. The analysis presented above would suggest that this should have been an active period for open market operations and the manipulation of reserve requirements. However, monetary policy as actually practised was quite different. One major instrument which was consistently used during the period was control over the lending of certain financial intermediaries, particularly over the lending of the clearing banks, i.e. Barclays, National Westminster, Midland, Lloyds, Williams and Glyns, Coutts and certain Scottish banks.

Such a policy raises two questions. First, how far, if at all, was the policy likely to be successful in curbing aggregate demand, and, secondly, what implications did it have for the allocative efficiency of the financial system? With regard to the first question, the effectiveness of a policy of controls on the lending activities of financial intermediaries obviously depended on the range of intermediaries over which such controls were exercised. If only the lending of a small group of intermediaries had been controlled, e.g. the banks, then borrowers could have turned to other groups as their sources of finance. This occurred to quite an extent during the 1960s in the United Kingdom. However, even if all intermediaries had been strictly controlled, this would not have implied effective control of aggregate demand. During the 1960s the authorities had rather loose control over the supply of money due to the way in which they managed the national debt (a topic taken up in Chapter 4). However, the point to be made here is that the authorities regarded money supply expansion as being consistent with restraining aggregate demand because they were controlling the outlets through which excess money balances could be channelled to borrowers, i.e. spenders. What might not have been appreciated, however, was that there were other ways in which economic units could have disposed of excess money holdings even with very strict control over most intermediaries. In the words of Meiselman (1969), the authorities might have believed that 'money was always to lend, never to spend'. The excess money could have been spent, instead of lent, to purchase equities, consumer durables, investment in human capital, and so on. Thus the effectiveness of a monetary policy concentrating purely on the lending powers of financial intermediaries might be doubted.

With regard to allocative efficiency, there are several objections to the system of monetary control described above. First, where some institutions were controlled and others not, it was inevitable that some inefficiencies would arise. Normally, borrowing would have been done from those institutions which were specialised in and most efficient at their particular forms of lending. If, however, an institution was unable to lend because of some particular restriction over its lending, borrowers would have had to turn to higher-cost uncontrolled institutions. Secondly, as a *quid pro quo* for direct controls on lending, the Bank of England condoned various oligopolistic practices in financial markets. The most important of these were the cartel agreements of the clearing banks whereby, among other things, the banks fixed borrowing and lending rates. The particular problems posed by a uniform lending rate with a quantitative limit on the quantity of loans were, of course, that the loans could not be rationed by price and, consequently, that it could not be certain that those loans which were made went to projects involving the greatest return.

Since monetary policy, as it was operated during this period, was open to such criticisms, we need to explore in more detail the justification of a policy that relies substantially on controlling the lending activities of a limited group of financial intermediaries. The rationale for this policy is contained in the Report of the Radcliffe Committee (1959), and broadly speaking it involved two notions. First, it is argued in the Report that money is a very close substitute for other financial assets, particularly those issued by non-bank financial intermediaries. The suggestion here is that following any monetary disturbance it would require only small changes in the returns on these financial assets to persuade economic units to hold willingly the changed money stock. For example, consider the case of a contractionary open-market operation. Economic units would now have too little money in relation to other financial assets at current returns. Their attempts at restoring equilibrium by exchanging some of these financial assets for money would result in driving down their prices and raising their returns. The important point, however, is that the Radcliffe Committee believed that only a very small increase in the returns of these financial assets would be required to restore equilibrium, i.e. to persuade economic units to hold less money.

A second belief of the Radcliffe Committee was that the demand for loan accommodation by borrowers from financial intermediaries is interest inelastic, so that increases in the cost of borrowing will have no great impact on reducing the demand for loans. The combination of these two notions suggests that the idea of monetary policy in the traditional sense of open-market operations and so on is unlikely to be effective. For example, following a contractionary monetary disturbance, economic units will demand only slightly more return for holding the liabilities of non-bank financial intermediaries. Such a rise in the cost of funds will be passed on to the borrowers of funds, but, since the rise is small and borrowers are not affected by the cost of funds to any great extent anyway, there is not likely to be much of a reduction in the amount of lending done. The Report then argues that the only effective instrument of control of the authorities is direct control over the lending of certain financial intermediaries. The Committee realised that using monetary control of this kind is likely to conflict with efficiency in the financial system, for similar reasons to those given above, e.g. the incentive given to turn to uncontrolled intermediaries. It is accordingly argued by the Committee that monetary policy should not be used as an instrument to control aggregate demand except in 'exceptional circumstances'. It appears that 'exceptional circumstances' prevailed throughout the 1960s.

The late 1960s witnessed some change of thinking on these matters and some dissatisfaction with monetary policy as it had been conducted in the post-Radcliffe era. The arguments of the Radcliffe Committee, which rejected traditional monetary policy, e.g. open market operations, had increasingly been questioned. First, it was argued that money may not have been such a close substitute for the liabilities of non-bank financial intermediaries as the Committee had thought. This meant that, following a monetary disturbance, a larger change in the returns of the liabilities of financial intermediaries would have been required to restore equilibrium. That is, the range of money substitutes that the Committee considered relevant was considered to be too narrow. Secondly, there was growing dissatisfaction with the allocative efficiency implications of the policy of direct controls on the lending activities of the banks. Since bank lending was controlled, banks had less incentive to compete for deposits, and, as mentioned above, as a *quid pro quo* for direct controls on bank lending the authorities condoned certain oligopolistic practices, e.g. interest rate agreements, in the banking industry. This dissatisfaction with the non-competitive behaviour of the banking system was expressed in two important reports of the 1960s, namely, the Prices and Incomes Board Report on *Bank Charges* and the Monopolies Commission Report on the proposed merger of Barclays and Lloyds. The culmination of these dissatisfactions was the publication of several papers by the Bank of England (1971, 1971a) setting out proposals for a new direction in monetary policy. The proposals consisted of two related parts.

First, there was to be a reorientation of the instruments of monetary policy. In the place of the earlier credit ceilings the main technique was the use of a uniform reserve requirement imposed across the *whole* of the banking system, where reserve assets were defined, broadly speaking, as certain public sector debt (e.g. balances at the Bank of England, Treasury bills, local authority bills and gilt-edged securities with a maturity of up to one year) and certain private sector assets. The methods by which the authorities intended to influence the total was through the use of open market operations in government securities and by the use of what was essentially a variable reserve requirement, i.e. special deposits. As mentioned above, the new reserve ratio, which was to be $12\frac{1}{2}$ per cent of eligible deposit liabilities, was applied across the whole of the banking system in an attempt to cast the net of control more widely.

The second major aim of the reforms, which were instituted in September 1971, was to move towards a financial system that was more allocatively efficient. More specifically, it was to reduce the distortions imposed on the financial system caused by the operation of monetary policy. In order to bring this about the direct controls over lending were scrapped, the collective interest rate agreements of the clearing banks were abandoned, and the above-mentioned uniform reserve ratio was also meant to contribute towards this aim. Little need be said about the scrapping of direct controls and the abandonment of interest rate agreements; both were useful changes as far as efficiency was concerned. However, it may be questioned whether just abandoning the *explicit* price fixing, i.e. interest rate agreements, was enough in a situation where the structure of the banking industry was so (and indeed remains so) oligopolistic. In such an industry the possibility existed that the *explicit* agreements would merely be replaced by *implicit* agreements. This may suggest that the policy should have been supplemented by policies that encouraged entry into banking or, if significant economies to scale existed, bank nationalisation.

However, the major question mark hangs over reserve ratios. The justification for reserve ratios is the ease of monetary control that they allow. Yet there are those who argue that monetary control is quite possible without the official imposition of such ratios. All that is basically required for monetary control is that reserve ratios do not move erratically. Under a system without official reserve ratios, the quantity of 'reserve' assets that intermediaries would wish to hold would be determined by the cost of holding them, the probability of deposit withdrawals and the particular intermediaries' attitude to risk. The argument then is that there is no real reason to believe that, in the absence of official dictation, self-imposed reserve ratios will be unstable. Furthermore, while not being necessary for monetary control, reserve requirements are a form of inefficiency. It was mentioned above that it is useful to regard reserve requirements as a form of taxation on the intermediaries concerned. There are two separate kinds of inefficiency caused by such taxation to be borne in mind. To begin with, even if all intermediaries were taxed equally (not equivalent to equal reserve requirements), this would reduce the amount of intermediation taking place. This is analogous to a tax on any product; that is, the output of a taxed product tends to be reduced. Secondly, we can envisage differential taxes on different classes of intermediaries. This would create distortions within the financial system;

some intermediaries (the lightly taxed) would expand, taking the business that would normally be done more cheaply by the other intermediaries (the more heavily taxed).

It may be thought that the 1971 UK policy change (the new policy is commonly referred to as Competition and Credit Control) excludes the second kind of inefficiency mentioned above, since all banks now face the same reserve requirements. This is not so, however. Intermediaries are implicitly taxed because they are forced to hold lower yielding assets than they would otherwise normally do. Therefore, a reserve requirement that makes intermediaries hold the same proportion of reserve assets only imposes an equal tax if, before the reserve requirement, they would have held the same amount of voluntary reserve assets. To take an example, namely, the merchant banks and the clearing banks, because of the different types of business that they carry on an equal 12½ per cent official reserve ratio militates against the former. Why is this so? Merchant banks deal in large deposits and make large loans, with little worry about deposits being withdrawn at short notice. Consequently, their balance sheets tend to be 'matched'; that is, if they have a lending possibility that offers a profit they match this loan by competing for an equal-sized (and termed) deposit on the market. As a result they have very little need for the assets that comprise the reserve requirement – assets which offer a lower return than that which they earn in their normal business – yet they are obliged to hold 12½ per cent of their liabilities in the form of such assets. On the other hand, the clearing banks, dealing as they do in retail banking, must remain more liquid to meet their more frequent demands for cash. As a result the reserve requirement imposes a larger implicit tax on the merchant banks than it does on the clearers.

INDICATORS OF MONETARY POLICY

Macroeconomic policy, as outlined in Chapter 1, is concerned with the manipulation of certain instrumental variables to affect target variables in the hope of moving them to some desired level. In that chapter we distinguished between primary instrumental variables and intermediate instrumental variables, where the former are those over which the authorities have fairly direct control. The latter lie between the primary instruments and the ultimate target variables. The intermediate instruments are affected by the primary instruments and in their turn affect the ultimate target variables. Examples of primary instruments in the field of monetary policy are given by open market operations and variation in reserve requirements. However, relatively recently there has been much discussion about the selection of the 'correct' intermediate instrumental variable of monetary policy. In the literature, instead of the term 'intermediate instrument', the term 'indicator variable' is used, i.e. a variable that indicates the correct thrust of monetary policy upon the particular target variable under consideration. One reason that such indicators are required is the lack of accurate quantitative information about the effect of policy changes.

The two major candidates to serve as monetary policy indicators are some measure of the money supply or of the rate of interest. To a large extent the choice depends, as Poole (1970) has shown, on whether or not the real sector of the economy is more stable than the monetary sector. For example, assume instability in the real sector and stability in the monetary sector. Let the instability in the real sector take the form of volatile shifts in investment which business would like to undertake, due to volatile changes in their expectations. Consider the case when they wish to invest more. Normally this would result in rising interest rates which would choke off part of the increase in investment demand. However, suppose the authorities, in an attempt to prevent interest rates from rising, increase the money supply to allow the financial system to meet the increased demand at unchanged rates. In this case aggregate demand will increase unchecked and give an expansion in economic activity. Consequently, the unchanged interest rates give an incorrect indication of the thrust of policy.

Suppose, however, that it is the monetary side of the economy that is the unstable sector, due to shifts in the demand for money balances. Consider the case in which the demand for money falls, e.g. due to the sudden introduction of credit cards. Economic units now have excess money balances which they will want to exchange for other assets, forcing up the prices of these assets and lowering their returns. This results in an expansionary effect on the economy, and it has been described earlier. In this case, although the supply of money has not changed, the interest rate will have fallen. Consequently, in the case of monetary sector instability the best indicator of policy thrust is the interest rate, not the change in the supply of money.

Chapter 4

Debt Management Policy

Debt management policy straddles two of the other main areas of economic policy, namely, fiscal policy and monetary policy. The need for the management of the debt in the first place arises from the deficits and surpluses of fiscal policy, and the way in which it is managed has important implications for the authorities' overall strategy with regard to monetary policy.

In this chapter we set out to examine certain aspects of the debt-financing problem. We begin by looking at the various ways in which the debt can be financed. In particular we look at the notion of the 'external financing of the public sector' and at the various instruments against which the government borrows. This leads us to an examination of some of the various aims that have been attached to debt management policy. This examination is carried out with reference to both UK and US experience. For example, during much of the 1960s the attitude of the UK authorities towards investors' expectations (or at least what the authorities thought investors' expectations were) and their subsequent response to investors' behaviour in the gilt-edged market led to a situation in which they surrendered control, to a large extent, over the supply of money.

The US authorities, on the other hand, have from time to time undertaken novel debt management policies, the most famous of which was perhaps the policy, carried out in the early 1960s, that became known as 'Operation Twist'. As we shall see later, Operation Twist was an attempt at simultaneously reducing interest rates on long term securities and raising those on short term securities. The reduction in the long term rates was desired in the hope that such a change would boost private investment and alleviate a high level of unemployment, whereas the rise in short term rates, it was hoped, would improve the capital account of the balance of payments. Since the success or otherwise of a policy like Operation Twist depends upon which factors are most important in determining the term structure of interest rates, we shall later spend some time reviewing the main theories of the term structure of interest rates and their respective implications for debt management policy.

FINANCING THE DEBT

Assume that the decisions have been taken for the amount of government expenditure to be carried out in a particular period and that the amount of revenue from taxation is known; the resulting balance is known simply as the consolidated fund balance. Combining this with the amount of loans made to the nationalised industries and to the local authorities gives the total of government expenditures and revenues. Should the final position be one in which the total of expenditures differs from revenues, the difference represents the amount that the authorities must raise from other sources and is known as the borrowing requirement. If expenditures exceed revenues this requirement is positive; if revenues exceed expenditures it is negative. It should be noted that part of the authorities' requirements is a need to finance existing debt, in the sense that existing debt instruments purchased in the past are continually being presented for redemption. In other words, as well as the possible need to finance current budgetary deficits, the authorities are also bound to a certain extent by past debt operations.

Before we examine the ways in which the borrowing requirement is met from domestic sources, we must explain how part of it may be financed by the foreign sector, i.e. the so-called 'external financing of the public sector'. Over a particular period domestic residents will be demanding foreign exchange (and supplying sterling in exchange) in order to purchase imports, make transfers and undertake various investments abroad. Similarly, foreigners will be demanding sterling (and supplying foreign exchange) in order to purchase UK exports, make transfers and undertake various investments in the United Kingdom. If the position is such that there is an excess supply of sterling and if the authorities do not wish the price of sterling (in terms of foreign currency, i.e. the exchange rate) to fall, they will be purchasing the excess supply of sterling and providing foreign currencies in exchange. (See Chapter 6 for a fuller discussion of the foreign exchange market.) The sterling thus received by the authorities constitutes finance for the public sector and therefore reduces the amount of borrowing that the authorities must undertake from other quarters. On the other hand, if there is an excess demand for sterling the authorities will be net purchasers of foreign exchange, providing sterling in return. The sterling required for such purchases of foreign exchange thus adds to the borrowing requirement.

Given the effect of the country's economic transactions with foreigners on the borrowing requirement, our attention must turn to the various methods by which the authorities borrow. Various kinds of classification may be applied to the debt that the authorities issue against themselves, namely, interest-bearing as opposed to non-interest-bearing debt, or marketable as opposed to non-marketable debt, or a classification of debt instruments in respect of their terms to maturity.

Perhaps the simplest way in which the government's requirements are met is through the issue of notes and coins. Such an issue constitutes what is, in effect, interest-free borrowing by the authorities. The quantity of currency (notes and coins) in circulation, however, is mainly determined by the economy's transactions needs and as such is not used as an instrument of policy.

Finance is also provided to the authorities by the issue of what is commonly known as non-marketable debt, which is represented by various national savings schemes and the public's purchases of premium bonds. From time to time the conditions of purchase are made more attractive in an effort to induce the public to take up larger amounts of such debt. For example, the variations that take place in the number and values of premium bond prizes are such attempts.

Finally we come to the types of marketable debt that are of prime importance in the management of the debt. The main distinction to be made with regard to these different forms of marketable debt is their term to maturity. At one extreme there exist short term bills (Treasury bills) which run for approximately three months from the date of issue and are issued weekly to provide for the residual needs of the government. Moving towards the other extreme we see longer-dated bonds of various maturities (gilt-edged securities) until we eventually reach a particular form of non-redeemable debt, namely, consols.

MONETARY IMPLICATIONS OF FINANCING THE DEBT

The impact that the debt-financing operation has on the supply of money in the economic system depends upon both the kind of debt issued and who takes up the debt.

If a government deficit is covered by an issue of marketable debt that is taken up by the non-bank private sector there will be no effect on the supply of money. As those in the non-bank private sector draw down their bank deposits in order to purchase the government securities, there will be a transfer of cash from the banks to the Treasury's account at the Bank of England. However, as the government spends the proceeds of their sale of securities, cash is transferred back to the private sector, and, as it is eventually deposited with the banks, their cash reserves are restored, leaving no overall effect (of the sale of securities) on the supply of money. It should be noted that the sale of securities to the non-bank private sector implies that the authorities are prepared to accept the rise in interest rates that will result. The government is in competition with other borrowers for the funds of the non-bank private sector, and consequently they must pay higher yields if they are to induce this sector to place their funds with them. If the authorities are unable to accept the rise in rates that would result if the non-bank private sector were totally to cover the deficit, the government must find at least some of the finance elsewhere.

One such alternative source of finance is for the authorities simply to increase the amount of currency in circulation. This will, however, lead to an increase in the supply of money directly. Similarly, if the authorities issue marketable securities which they sell to the Bank of England, increasing the Treasury's account at that bank, this also will have the effect of increasing the supply of money. As the government spends the money, private-sector bank deposits (and the cash reserves of the banks) rise, allowing a multiple expansion of bank lending.

Finally, the banking sector itself may provide some of the financing needs of the government by purchasing various kinds of government debt. Here the effect on the supply of money will differ according to the kind of government securities acquired by the banks. If they acquire short term bills (Treasury bills) which constitute part of the banks' reserve assets (see Chapter 3), there is likely to be room for some multiple expansion of bank lending. The acquisition of other kinds of marketable debt by the banks, e.g. long term securities, will only cause a once-and-for-all rise in the deposit base of the banking system.

The important point, therefore, is that the more willing the authorities are to accept rises in interest rates in order to cover the deficit by borrowing from the non-bank private sector, the smaller will be the impact of a given government deficit on the supply of money. By the same token, the less willing the authorities are to see interest rates rise, the more they will have to have recourse to other sources of finance which result in upward pressure on the supply of money.

AIMS OF DEBT MANAGEMENT POLICY

So far we have examined the need, on the part of the authorities, to issue debt to finance the government's borrowing requirement over a particular period and the various kinds of debt against which the authorities borrow. However, the debt issued to finance the deficit of one particular year, say, represents a small proportion of the total of outstanding debt – a total which is the result of government borrowing in the past. This total of outstanding debt may be expanded or contracted as the result of current fiscal policy (i.e.

whether the government has currently a positive or negative borrowing requirement) or of government sales or purchases of existing debt (e.g. a Bank of England open-market sale of existing securities which aims at reducing the supply of money).

With all this in mind we turn our attention to some possible aims that the authorities may have in their management of the debt, using examples from UK and US experience as illustration.

UK debt management experience

In the postwar period the United Kingdom has had a large amount of outstanding debt as the result of borrowing to finance the Second World War and the nationalisation that followed it. This large amount of outstanding debt required finance to service it – finance which was in addition to the finance required to cover future government budgetary deficits. Consequently, it was the view of the authorities that their main aim in their management of the debt should be to ensure that future government borrowing could be undertaken without undesirably large rises in interest rates. Furthermore, the authorities wished that, as far as possible, the borrowing should be undertaken by issuing long term (gilt-edged) securities rather than by issuing short term (Treasury) bills.

There are a number of reasons for the authorities' desire to concentrate their borrowing at the longer end of market. First, the greater the amount of long term debt that investors were willing to absorb, the less need there was to have recourse to short term borrowing from the banking system. This was desirable since, as explained in the previous section, short term finance from the banks involves upward pressure on the supply of money. Secondly, as mentioned in the Radcliffe Committee Report, the larger the proportion of longer term debt, the less likely it was that the Treasury would be embarrassed by maturing claims at inconvenient moments.

We have seen then that the main aim of the UK authorities in their management of the debt was to encourage investors to purchase gilt-edged securities. It was their belief that in order to achieve this they should actively intervene in the gilt-edged market, to prevent violent fluctuations in interest rates. The authorities viewed the market as being dominated by investors who had short planning horizons, i.e. by investors who were to a large measure particularly interested in making short term gains where possible. This meant that whereas *high rates* (low bond prices) induced a higher demand for bonds, rising rates (falling prices) caused a reduction in demand (a shift of the demand curve for bonds). This was believed to be so since it was the contention of the authorities that investors' expectations of how bond rates were to move in the near future were formed upon their experience in the recent past – more precisely, that investors extrapolated past movements in rates rather than believed in a return to a 'normal' rate. Such dynamic considerations in the function for bonds, in the absence of counter-speculating on the supply side by the authorities, would, it was thought, lead to rather sharp movements in interest rates. As aiready mentioned, this was exactly what the authorities did not wish to happen. Consequently, they took up a counter-speculating stance, standing ready to buy stocks on a falling market, i.e. falling gilt-edged prices. However, it should not be thought that the authorities' intention was to pin rates. Rather, their stated policy was that 'the daily concern of debt management is usually to steady the market without opposing it too rigidly' (Bank of England, 1966). This steadying of the market was bought at a price, however. That price was the extent to which control over the supply of money was surrendered. In supporting the market by buying back stock when prices were falling, they were in effect boosting the reserve base of the banks, which were then in a position to expand credit. That is, by buying back stock they were invariably providing cash in return, which increased the reserve base of the banking system. However, as noted in Chapter 3, they attempted to counter this by imposing direct controls on the lending of the banking system.

Towards the end of the 1960s there was a marked change of emphasis in the authorities' attitude towards the gilt-edged market. They became less willing to support the market and began to allow variations in investors' appetites for medium and long term gilts to be reflected in their yields. As mentioned in Chapter 3, this was a period during which some rethinking was going on about the conduct of monetary policy. This rethinking culminated in the introduction of Competition and Credit Control in September 1971 which, among other changes, intended that policy should be moved towards the control of the 'broader monetary aggregates'. Essentially, it represented a move towards stricter control over the supply of money. Our present concern is with the more positive approach to the gilt-edged market that this change implied. This more positive approach to the gilt-edged market is neatly summed up in the words of the then Governor of the Bank of England (Bank of England, 1971a):

'It was, moreover, important for the working of the new system that we should reduce the extent of our intervention in the long-term gilt market. For this reason we announced on the 14th May that the Bank of England no longer felt obliged to provide, as in the past, outright support for the gilt-edged market in stocks having a maturity of over one year . . . Thus we shall not normally be prepared to facilitate movements out of gilt-edged by the banks, even if their sales should cause the market temporarily to weaken sharply.'

'Pure' debt management policy

We now turn to what may be described as 'pure' debt management policy. By 'pure' debt policy we refer to action taken that aims to alter the composition of outstanding debt but does not affect its total volume. A 'pure' debt policy that lengthens the average maturity of outstanding debt is referred to as *funding*; one that shortens the average maturity of the debt is an *unfunding* operation. What may the aim of a pure debt policy be?

The authorities may wish to conduct a pure debt policy in order to alter the structure of interest rates. For example, they may wish to lower the long term rate for the purposes of domestic expansion (because investment is thought to be more sensitive to changes in the long rate than to those in the short rate) while simultaneously raising the short rate for the purposes of external equilibrium, i.e. to induce a large net inflow (or a smaller net outflow) of funds on the capital account of the balance of payments. To this end, the authorities would purchase long term debt and replace it with an equivalent amount of short term debt. Whether or not such a policy could begin to be successful would depend on what determines the term structure of interest rates, and it is to an examination of the main term-structure theories that we must now turn.

THEORIES OF THE TERM STRUCTURE OF INTEREST RATES

At the outset it is essential for the reader to be clear about what exactly economists mean when they refer to the 'term structure of interest rates'.

Interest yields on various kinds of debt may differ for a variety of reasons. Perhaps the most obvious factor causing a difference of yields is the amount of risk associated with each kind of debt, i.e. the risk of default in the payment of interest and the repayment of principal upon redemption. Another factor of some importance is the extent to which holdings of various kinds of debt are accompanied by various tax exemptions.

However, these considerations apart, an interesting phenomenon is the relationship between the yields on 'safe' securities which differ only in their terms to maturity. The relationship between the yields on various securities and their terms to maturity is referred to as a yield curve. The shape of the yield curve indicates the term structure of interest rates. Historically, there have been a number of patterns. Some periods have witnessed rising yield curves (i.e. securities of longer maturities have higher yields than securities of shorter maturities); others have witnessed falling yield curves, and yet others flat or humped yield curves. Flat yield curves indicate that securities of all maturities have the same yield, and humped yield curves indicate that yields on securities are successively higher up to a certain maturity and are thereafter successively lower.

Basically, there are two theories (and a number of variants of these) which attempt to explain why the yield curve is shaped as it is at different periods of time. These two fundamental theories are known as the Expectations Theory and the Hedging (or Institutional) Theory. We shall see that these two approaches have critically different implications for the success of a debt policy that changes the supplies of different debt instruments in an attempt to alter the shape of the yield curve. We therefore begin with an outline of the Expectations Theory.

Expectations Theory

The assumptions of the extreme form of the Expectations Theory are as follows:

(1) The 'safe' securities of various maturities (mentioned above) are perfect substitutes in the portfolios of investors.
(2) Investors are profit maximisers whose only consideration is to hold that composition of financial assets in their portfolios which will maximise return over a particular holding period.
(3) All investors hold, with certainty, the same expectations of how future rates are going to behave.

Given these assumptions, the shape of the yield curve will be determined by what investors' expectations of the future are. If investors in general believe solidly that future short rates will rise, they will curtail their current demand for long-dated securities (pushing up their yields) and move into short-dated securities (depressing their yields), giving a resultant upward-sloping yield curve.

There are two reasons that would lead lenders to undertake such a switch. If rates on short and long-dated securities are the same and the expectation is that future rates will rise, investors will wish to hold shorts, since they will soon be redeemed and the principal reinvested at the higher expected rate. Secondly, if future rates do rise as expected, those holding long debt will be subjected to a capital loss. The behaviour of borrowers (the issuers of debt) will also tend to push up long yields and pull down short yields, since, if rates are expected to rise, long term borrowers will wish to retire their shorter obligations and take advantage of the current low long rates.

Making use of some simple algebra, we can attempt to formalise the extreme version of the Expectations Theory. Let R stand for an actual current rate and r for an expected future rate. Because we must inevitably deal with different time periods and a variety of maturities, let a pre-subscript represent the period to which the rate applies and a post-subscript refer to the maturity of the bond to which the rate refers. Thus, for example, ${}_1R_2$ represents the rate on a bond in period 1 (i.e. the current period) having a maturity of two years, and ${}_3r_1$ represents the expected rate on one-year bonds that will be effective in period 3.

For simplicity, let us consider the case of an investor who has funds of £1 to invest over the next two years. Security purchases which are available to him are either one two-year bond or two one-year bonds. If he chooses the first investment, this will be worth $(1+{}_1R_2)^2$ pounds to him at the end of the two years. On the other hand, if he decides on the second investment, he will invest in a one-year bond now, collecting $(1+{}_1R_1)$ pounds at the end of the first year. This he will reinvest at the one-year rate that he expects to rule in the second year, namely, ${}_2r_1$. Therefore, by the second route he expects to collect $(1+{}_1R_1)(1+{}_2r_1)$ pounds at the end of the second year. In equilibrium, where there is no incentive for the investor to switch between securities, we must have

$$(1+{}_1R_2)^2=(1+{}_1R_1)(1+{}_2r_1) \tag{1}$$

If next year's expectation for the one-year rate, ${}_2r_1$, is higher than the current one-year rate, ${}_1R_1$, the current two-year rate, ${}_1R_2$, will be higher than ${}_1R_1$. This is so because investors will have expected to earn more by buying two consecutive short bonds than by holding the two-year issue. Consequently, the movement from the longer-dated issue to the shorter will have pushed up rates on the former and pulled down those on the latter. In short, the current two-year rate is a geometric average of the present one-year rate and the expected future one-year rate; that is,

$${}_1R_2=\sqrt{(1+{}_1R_1)\ (1+{}_2r_1)}-1 \tag{2}$$

We may take this principle a step further and consider an investment period of three years. By similar argument, in equilibrium we have

$$(1+{}_1R_3)^3=(1+{}_1R_1)(1+{}_2r_1)(1+{}_3r_1) \tag{3}$$

Substituting equation 1 into equation 3 gives

$$(1+{}_1R_3)^3=(1+{}_1R_2)^2\,(1+{}_3r_1) \tag{4}$$

If ${}_3r_1 > {}_2r_1$, then ${}_1R_3 > {}_1R_2$, and if ${}_3r_1 < {}_2r_1$, then ${}_1R_3 < {}_1R_2$. From equation 3 we have

$$ {}_1R_3 = \sqrt[3]{(1+{}_1R_1)(1+{}_2r_1)(1+{}_3r_1)} - 1 \quad (5)$$

Equation 5 merely carries the idea of equation 2 into another period. In general then for *n* periods ahead, we have

$$ {}_1R_n = \sqrt[n]{(1+{}_1R_1)(1+{}_2r_1)(1+{}_3r_1)\dots(1+{}_nr_1)} - 1 \quad (6)$$

The Expectations Theory then explains the structure of current market rates in terms of anticipated future yields on short term securities. If future short rates are expected to remain unchanged, the yield curve will be flat. If they are expected to be successively higher, the yield curve will be upward sloping; if successively lower, it will be downward sloping. The theory can even account for yield curves that have been observed first to rise and then to fall. According to this theory, this occurs if future short rates are expected first to rise and then to fall.

The proponents of this explanation of the term structure of interest rates hold out very little hope for the success of a 'pure' debt management policy that, without altering the overall total of outstanding debt, changes the average maturity of the debt in the hope that the rate structure can be twisted. Attempts at doing this require changes in the relative supplies of different kinds of debt. If the authorities wish to see a rise in short term rates and a fall in long term rates, they will replace a given amount of long term debt with an equivalent of short term debt. However, according to the Expectations Theory, outlined above, such a policy will have little or no impact on the structure of interest rates. The reason is quite simply that, since investors regard both long and short term debt as perfect substitutes in their portfolios, they will willingly reshuffle the composition of their portfolios to accommodate the change in relative supplies without any appreciable change in yields being required.

This may be illustrated with the use of Figures 4.1a and 4.1b, which depict the demand and supply of short and long term debt respectively. As we know already, an investor has a choice of many maturities of debt, but for purposes of illustration we have chosen only two classifications, namely, short and long term debt. This simplification does not alter the general conclusion. The demand for each class of debt is given as a function of yield, and, since by assumption of the Expectations Theory both classes of debt are perfect substitutes for each other, these demand curves are drawn with infinite elasticity. The original supplies are given as S_s and S_l.

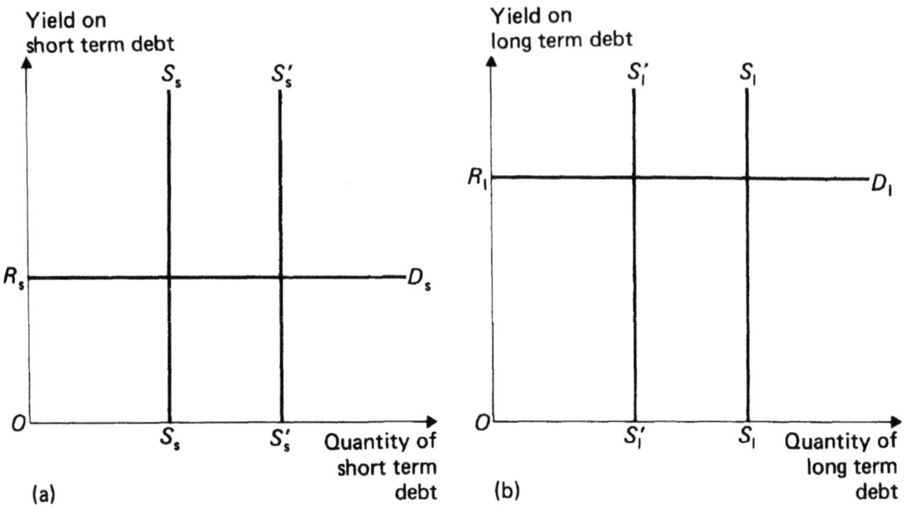

Figure 4.1 *The effect of a 'pure' debt management policy on the structure of interest rates under the expectations theory*

We begin by assuming that the long rate lies above the short rate. According to the Expectations Theory, this must be due solely to the fact that the future short rate is expected to be higher than the current short rate. Suppose that the authorities wish to retire $(S_l - S_l')$ of long debt and replace it with $(S_s' - S_s)$ of short debt. As is illustrated in Figures 4.1a and 4.1b, this can be done without any change in the relative yields of the two kinds of debt. The only possibility of the yields being affected is if the change in relative supplies affects investors' expectations of the behaviour of future short rates.

Hedging (or Institutional) Theory

The second basic approach to the determination of the term structure of interest rates – an approach which is at the opposite extreme from the Expectations Theory – is referred to by a number of different titles, namely, the Institutional, Hedging or Segmentation approach. The essence of this approach is that investors are much averse to risk. As a result they will hedge against risks by matching the maturity of their assets with that of their liabilities. If an investor is in a position where the maturity of his assets is longer than that of his liabilities, he puts himself into a position of a possible capital loss when he is forced to sell his assets before they become due for redemption. For example, consider an individual who has borrowed £100 for a period of one year; that is, his £100 liability has a maturity of one year. Suppose also that with this sum of £100 he buys a security that is due for redemption in ten years' time;

that is, his asset has a maturity of ten years. However, as he must pay back the £100 loan after one year, he runs the risk that when he comes to sell his asset after one year its price will have fallen below £100 and he will have suffered a capital loss. To avoid this possible capital loss he could have purchased an asset with a one-year maturity, matching that of his liability, and so be certain of receiving £100 to repay the loan.

On the other hand, if an investor has assets of shorter maturity than that of his liabilities, he runs the risk of income loss. To illustrate this case, let us take the example of an individual who borrows £100 for two years with which he purchases a security having a maturity of one year. After the first year he receives back the £100 plus an interest payment. However, at this stage he still has one year before he must repay his loan, and consequently he makes an investment for a further year. If interest rates have fallen in the meantime, he runs the risk that his total interest payments on his investments over the two years will be lower than if he had merely invested the £100 by buying a two-year security. This risk is the risk of incurring an income loss. Those who subscribe to the Hedging Theory believe that the majority of investors practise what is commonly known as 'matching'. That is, to avoid the two kinds of risk dealt with above, investors match the maturities of their assets and liabilities.

The thrust of the institutionalists' argument is to give examples of large market-participating institutions whose preferences for different maturities will vary according to the kind of business that they undertake. Thus insurance companies and pension funds, for example, which have long term obligations (liabilities), will be attracted mainly towards long term assets. On the other hand, commercial banks, for example, which place great emphasis on liquidity, will prefer to concentrate on the shorter end of the market. The upshot of these attitudes is that there is a certain amount of non-substitutability between maturities. The Hedging Theory therefore sees the market rates on securities of different maturities as being determined by separate conditions of demand and supply in each maturity. Across the maturity spectrum we must envisage, according to this approach, a number of separate and insulated markets.

Proponents of this view of the determination of the term structure of interest rates feel that the kind of 'pure' debt policy that we have mentioned can be successful in twisting the structure of interest rates. Figures 4.2a and 4.2b illustrate why this is so. The components of these figures are similar to those of Figures 4.1a and 4.1b. One crucial difference, of course, is that the demand schedules for long and short term debt are of less than infinite

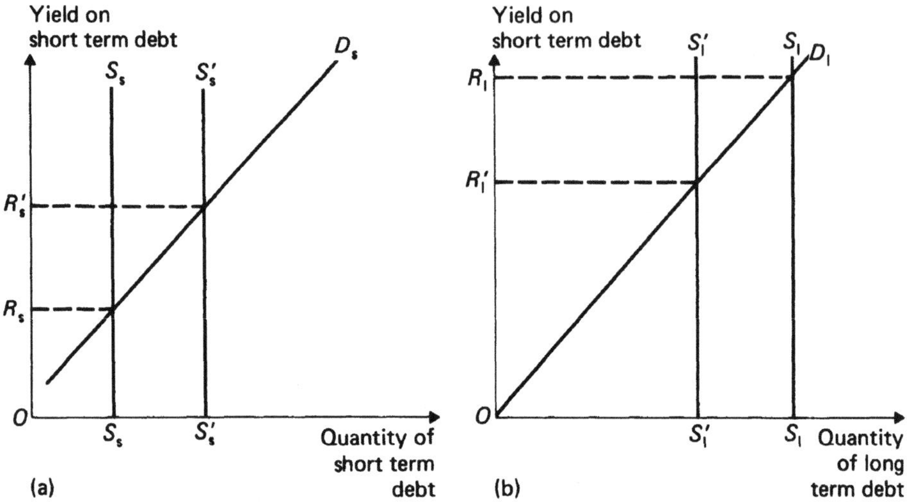

Figure 4.2 *The effect of a 'pure' debt management policy on the structure of interest rates under the hedging theory*

elasticity with respect to rates. This is so since the two kinds of debt are less than perfectly substitutable. If we conduct the same exercise as in Figures 4.1a and 4.1b, i.e. of retiring $(S_l - S_l')$ of long debt and replacing it with $(S_s' - S_s)$ of short debt, we find that the spread between the rates has been reduced.

THE EXPERIENCE OF 'OPERATION TWIST'

We conclude this chapter by examining the results of an experiment in debt policy which took place in the United States in the early 1960s. The US economy emerged from the 1950s with the dual problem of domestic unemployment and a large deficit on the balance of payments. A general expansionary policy, aimed at alleviating the underutilisation of domestic resources, would only have aggravated the problem on external account. Not only would the trade balance have deteriorated due to an increased consumption of imports, but in addition the falling interest rates that would have resulted from the expansionary policy would have caused added deterioration of the capital account.

In order to attack the joint problem the US authorities attempted to conduct a policy that would have pushed up short rates (to affect the external position) and pulled down long rates (to affect domestic investment). To this end they attempted to retire an amount of long term debt and replace it with short debt in a policy that, as mentioned earlier, became known as 'Operation Twist'. As noted by Ross (1966), the twisting of the yield structure was a *necessary* but not a *sufficient* condition for the success of the policy. Whereas the fall in the long rate might have been expected to have a favourable impact on fixed investment, it was possible that the rise in the short rate would have depressed the desire to undertake investment in inventory stocks. Consequently, the overall effect could have been to cause a reduction in total domestic investment – the opposite, in fact, of what the policy was meant to achieve. Ross uses various estimates, from past studies, of the short and long interest-rate elasticities of inventory and fixed investment respectively, in an attempt to make a judgement of what likely overall effect on total investment the twist policy had. He concludes that in only two of the six cases that he considers could the policy have been successful in increasing domestic investment and therefore in reducing the level of unemployment. The reader should note that, for a satisfactory resolution of this point, knowledge of two further elasticities are required, namely, the extent to which the short and long rates will move in response to a given change in the relative supplies of short and long term securities.

With regard to whether the policy was successful in twisting the structure of rates in the first place, opinions differ here also. During the years following the introduction of the policy the spread between the short and long rates did in fact narrow. However, it has been pointed out by Malkiel (1973) that this was not due to any conscious policy on behalf of the authorities. He emphasises that while the Federal Reserve Bank (the US central bank) was attempting to replace long term securities in the hands of the public with short term issues – a policy that he also remarks 'was never pursued with much vigour . . . the Treasury was attempting to lengthen the maturity structure of the debt through a policy of "advanced refunding" '. Malkiel then concludes:

'In the net, the changes in the maturity composition of the debt were actually perverse. Instead of shortening the debt structure, as was called for by the policy objective, it was actually somewhat lengthened. What limited success the policy had probably resulted from its "announcement effect" on investors' expectations. The US experience with Operation Twist, therefore, cannot be used to support the view that it is impossible for monetary authorities to alter the shape of the yield curve appreciably.'

Modigliani and Sutch (1966, 1967), while agreeing with Malkiel that the actions of the Federal Reserve and Treasury could not take the credit for the narrowing of the spread between rates, on the other hand explain the events of the period 1961–5 by their development of a theory of the term structure of interest rates, which they call the preferred Habitat Theory. Their theory is based on the assumption that different investors have different 'preferred habitats' according to the pattern of their liabilities. However, the possibility exists that investors may be tempted out of their habitats if 'other maturities (longer or shorter) offer an expected premium sufficient to compensate for the risk and cost of moving out of one's habitat'. Modigliani and Sutch (1966) state:

'Under this model the rate for a given maturity, *n*, could differ from the rate implied by the Pure Expectations Hypothesis by positive or negative "risk premiums" reflecting the extent to which the supply of funds with habitat *n* differs from the aggregate demand for *n* period loans forthcoming at that rate. If the *n* period demand exceeded the funds with *n* period habitat, there would tend to arise a premium in the *n* period maturity, and conversely. Such premiums or discounts would tend to bring about shifts in funds between different maturity markets, both through the "speculation" of investors tempted out of their natural habitat by the lure of higher expected returns and through "arbitrage" by intermediaries induced to "take a position" by borrowing in the maturity range where the expected return is low, and lending where the expected return is high.'

Using this approach, Modigliani and Sutch go on to present their explanation of why the spread between short and long rates narrowed during the period when Operation Twist was being carried out. They explain that changes occurred which enabled potential arbitrageurs to attract more short term funds which they then invested in longer term securities, pulling down the rates on these. These arbitrageurs were the commercial banks, and the changes in question were successive relaxations of Regulation Q. Regulation Q constitutes a control on US commercial banks whereby an upper limit is placed on the rate that they may pay in order to attract time deposits (the US equivalent of UK deposit accounts). A raising of this upper limit would presumably reduce the spread between the rates by allowing the banks to attract more short term funds and arbitrage away part of the premium payable on the longer securities. Relaxations of this upper limit took place twice during the period in question, namely, in the first quarter of 1962 and again in the last quarter of 1964.

Finally, a further development took place which added to Modigliani and Sutch's beliefs. This was the introduction in 1961 of negotiable Time Certificates of Deposit. These instruments brought increased benefits both to the banks and to the investors who purchased them with the funds they had available. As far as the banks were concerned, these deposits were placed for a fixed period, and because of this the banks were willing to pay higher rates for such deposits – something they were able to do due to the raising of ceiling rates under Regulation Q. Depositors also found such instruments attractive for two reasons: first, they paid a higher return than normal time deposits, and, secondly, their liquidity was increased due to their being negotiable.

Chapter 5

Prices and Incomes Policy

In the introductory chapter we mentioned some of the problems that persistent inflation poses for an economy. Such inflation has been a problem for most Western economies since the end of the Second World War. In the United Kingdom the average rate of price inflation in the postwar years up to 1967 was approximately 3 per cent. However, after 1967 it accelerated (as it did in other Western countries), becoming 5·4 per cent in 1969, 9·4 per cent in 1971, 16·1 per cent in 1974 and 24·2 per cent in 1975. Many of the governments concerned have felt constrained from attempting to deal with inflation solely with the use of demand management policies, i.e. monetary and fiscal policies, because of the belief that the level of unemployment this would entail would be unacceptably high. Instead, various policies under the general heading 'prices and incomes policy' have been attempted. While under this general heading many different policies have been used, they have the common characteristic that they have attempted to impose direct government control over incomes and prices, instead of leaving these to be determined by the workings of the free market.

Before analysing the role and likely effectiveness of prices and incomes policies in curtailing inflation, we need to have some understanding of what are regarded as the causes of inflation. Although there are many models attempting to explain the inflationary process, the one outlined below has been most commonly applied to the analysis of prices and incomes policies. The model will enable us to have some idea of what kind of policies are likely to be useful and how such policies are supposed to operate. We begin by looking at the determination of prices.

THE DETERMINATION OF PRICE CHANGES

In the idealised case of the competitive market, prices are determined by the forces of demand and supply. If, at the prevailing price, demand exceeds supply there will be a tendency for prices to rise and vice versa. In the special limiting case where there is instantaneous adjustment of price, supply and demand are kept in continuous equality.

One alternative view of price determination argues that, because of the oligopolistic structure of modern economies and the institutional character of modern corporate management, the important factors determining firms' behaviour in their price setting are the long term security and expansion of the firm. According to this view of price setting, if demand were to rise the burden of market adjustment would be borne by unsatisfied demanders, possibly involving some sort of rationing. If demand were to fall the adjustment would be borne by lower production. With this approach prices are determined by the considerations developed under the theory of 'full cost pricing'. That is, prices are set equal to the sum of average total cost plus a markup allowance for profits, or

$$P = (1+Z) \cdot C$$

where P is price per unit of output, C is average cost per unit of output and Z is the markup factor. The costs per unit consist of the sum of unit labour costs and unit material costs.

What determines the markup factor? If the markup factor is determined by the level of excess demand, then the full-cost pricing approach is not dissimilar from the conventional approach. It is argued, however, that the markup factor is based on conditions of market structure and the long run conditions of the industry. These include such factors as barriers to entry, level of concentration, degree of product differentiation and long-run demand elasticities. The full cost theory suggests that the following variables should affect prices: first, changes in costs, caused either by changes in prices of inputs or technological change, and, secondly, changes in the markup factor. However, the important point is that prices will not respond to changes in demand.

This list of factors affecting prices is different from those given by the conventional supply and demand approach. In that theory changes in prices are a function solely of excess demand. The effects of cost changes, which cause movements of the supply schedule, will be reflected in the one single explanatory variable, namely, excess demand.

What difference does the dichotomy between views of price determination, outlined above, make for our purposes? The major difference is that they have different implications for policies designed to attack inflation. If it is accepted that price determination is basically of the full cost variety, then appropriate anti-inflationary policies will be directed at controlling profit markups and major elements of costs, e.g. wages. On the other hand, if the excess demand view is held, then, besides the cost elements that affect the position of the supply schedule, demand factors must play a part, as must the size of the response of price to the level of excess demand.

Nearly all theoretical and empirical studies of the effect of prices and incomes policies on inflation have adopted, either explicitly or implicitly, the full-cost pricing hypothesis. This means that our attention must be focused on the possible effects of an incomes policy on profit markups and costs. Since labour costs are the largest portion of unit costs in many industries, attention has been paid to the problem of determining changes in labour costs.

THE DETERMINATION OF WAGE CHANGES

In our discussion of the determination of the prices of goods and services, we distinguished between a theory that saw price changes as depending upon the presence of excess demand and one that saw price changes as being caused mainly by cost changes. A similar distinction can be drawn with regard to wage determination.

Conventional supply and demand theory of wage determination would argue that the presence of excess demand would cause wages to rise, and vice versa. However, an assumption might also be made about the speed with which wages react to the existence of excess demand; namely, the greater is the extent of excess demand, the faster wages will rise. That is,

$$\frac{\Delta W}{W} = k \cdot \frac{D_L - S_L}{S_L} \qquad \text{(where } k > 0\text{)}$$

where W denotes wages and ΔW changes in wages, D_L and S_L represent the demand and supply of labour respectively, and k is greater than zero, reflecting the assumption mentioned above that the greater is excess demand the faster wages will rise.

These relationships of the conventional supply and demand theory of wage determination are shown, *for a particular labour market*, in Figure 5.1. (Later we assume that the above relationships for individual micro markets can be 'easily' aggregated to give macro-economic relationships. However, such aggregation is fraught with difficulties. See Peston (1971) for a discussion of the difficulties involved.) In Figure 5.1a the demand schedule for labour, $D_L D_L$, shows the amount of labour, Q_L, that firms desire to employ per unit of time, t, at each *money* wage rate the supply schedule of labour, $S_L S_L$, shows the number of workers offering themselves for employment at each money wage rate. The equilibrium wage rate, W_e, is given where supply equals demand. At wage rates above W_e there is excess supply of labour and so rates will tend to fall; at wage rates below W_e there is excess demand and so rates will begin to rise. Figure 5.1b shows more exactly this tendency for wages to change in the presence of excess demand. Along the

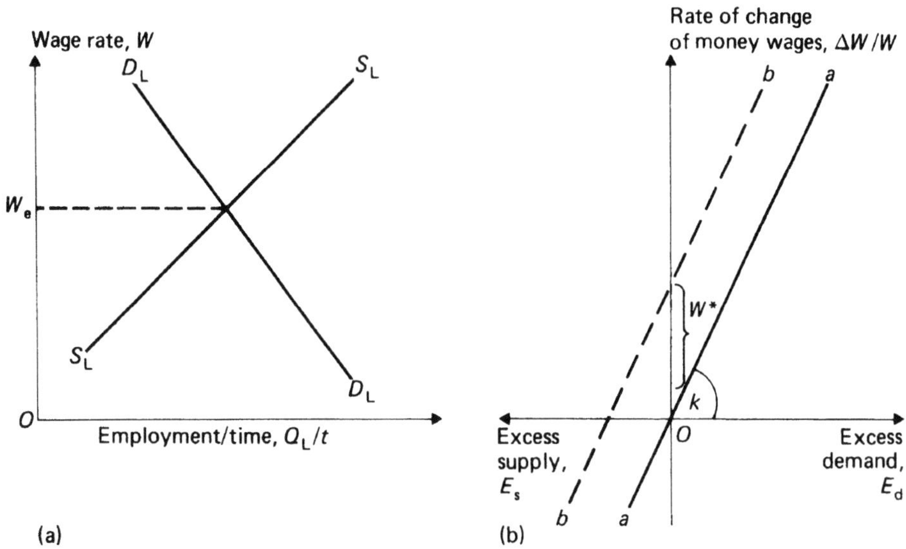

Figure 5.1 *Excess demand and the rate of wage inflation*

horizontal axis is measured the extent of excess demand, E_d, or of excess supply, E_s, while up the vertical axis is measured the rate of wage change, $\Delta W/W$. The function plotted, namely,

$$\frac{\Delta W}{W} = k \cdot \frac{D_L - S_L}{S_L}$$

shows the extent of wage adjustment to the corresponding level of excess demand. This function, commonly referred to as a *reaction function*, is labelled *aa*.

Unfortunately, empirical verification of the relationships assumed above is not a simple task, because direct observation of the demand and supply schedules if difficult. However, it is possible to approach the problem in a less direct manner. This is done by considering the frictions that are likely to exist in the labour market. If there were no frictions within any labour market, we should observe that the actual number of people employed would equal the supply of labour when the wage rate was below the equilibrium level and would equal the demand for labour when the wage rate was above equilibrium level. This means that the standard assumption is made that in disequilibrium situations the actual number of transactions, which in the case of the labour market means the number of people employed, is determined by the lesser of the quantity demanded or supplied. Therefore, we should observe either unemployment (when there is excess supply) or job vacancies (when there is excess demand), but we should not observe both job vacancies and unemployment in any particular labour market simultaneously.

However, this does not correspond to any labour market actually observed. The presence of both unemployment and vacancies in any particular labour market can be explained as the result of frictions. For example, any labour market will comprise, on the demand side, many firms. This means that some individuals will from time to time be changing employment. Unless we assume that people who resign or lose their jobs in one employment become immediately re-employed, given vacancies do exist, there will always be a certain irreducible minimum amount of frictional unemployment. What this means in terms of our supply and demand schedules for labour is that actual employment will *not* be on the supply schedule (if wages are below equilibrium) nor on the demand schedule (if wages are above equilibrium). Instead, actual employment will lie somewhere to the left of both the demand and supply schedules. Therefore, we may visualise a schedule that shows actual levels of employment at different wage rates. The question is: what relationship would this actual employment schedule have to the demand and supply schedules of Figure 5.1a? The most reasonable type of relationship between the schedule of the actual level of employment, *EE*, and the supply and demand curves is shown in Figure 5.2a. How can the position of this *EE* schedule be rationalised? Lipsey (1974) provides an answer: 'In any sort of search model we would expect the number of unemployed who find jobs each period to be an increasing function both of the number of persons searching for jobs and the number of jobs available.' Therefore, when the wage rate is below the equilibrium rate, the actual employment schedule, *EE*, will move nearer and nearer to the supply schedule, $S_L S_L$, the greater the extent of excess demand. That is, the more jobs there are available, the less likely it is that frictional unemployment will be substantial. Similarly, at wage rates above the equilibrium rate, the actual employment schedule, *EE*, will move closer to the demand schedule, $D_L D_L$, the larger is the extent of excess supply. That is, frictional unemployment will be smaller, the greater is the number of people searching for jobs.

If the actual employment schedule, *EE*, has the shape shown in Figure 5.2a, this allows us to derive a relationship between unemployment and excess demand for labour, as shown in Figure 5.2b. Such a relationship is derived as follows. (Remember that the level of unemployment is given by the distance between the actual employment schedule, *EE*, and the labour supply schedule, $S_L S_L$, and that the excess demand for labour is given by the distance between the labour supply and labour demand schedules.) Beginning with the wage rate W_1 in Figure 5.2a, we note that unemployment

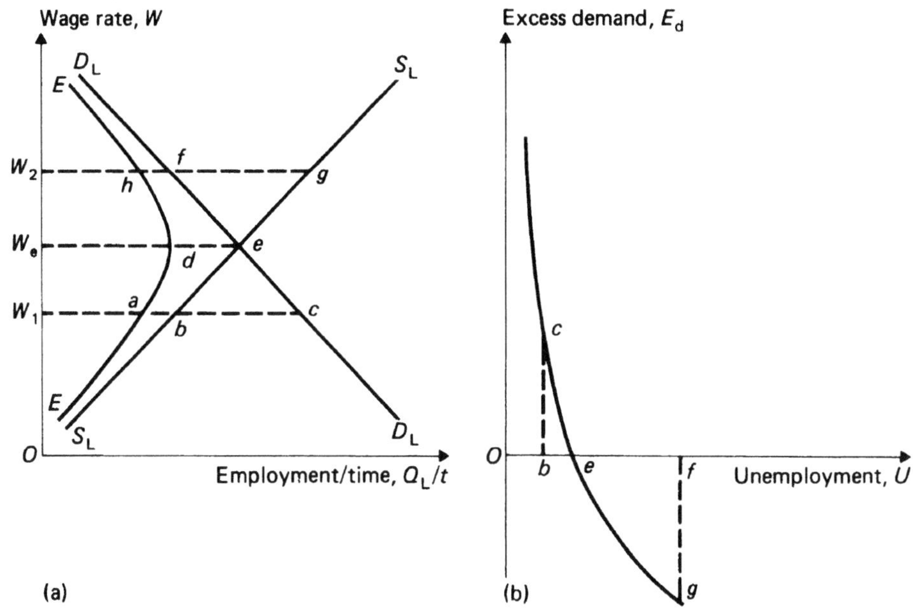

Figure 5.2 *Derivation of the excess demand-unemployment relationship*

is the distance *ab*, which is associated with a level of excess demand equal to distance *bc*. This relationship is plotted as point *c* in Figure 5.2b, where the level of excess demand, *bc*, is associated with unemployment *Ob*, where $Ob = ab$ of Figure 5.2a. As the wage rate rises above W_1 we note that the level of unemployment rises while excess demand falls, until wage rate W_e is reached. Here the level of unemployment is the distance *de*, which is associated with zero excess demand. Such a combination of these two variables is plotted as point *e* in Figure 5.2b, where $Oe = de$ of Figure 5.2a. As the wage rate rises above the level W_e, say to W_2, unemployment increases and excess supply appears. At wage rate W_2, the level of unemployment represented by distance *hg* is associated with an excess supply of labour equal to distance *fg*. This combination is plotted as point *g* in Figure 5.2b where $Of = hg$ of Figure 5.2a.

The relation between excess demand and unemployment in Figure 5.2b is therefore obtained by taking wage rates in Figure 5.2a and plotting the associated pairs of unemployment and excess demand that they imply. The excess demand–unemployment relation will have the shape shown in Figure 5.2b if the actual employment schedule, *EE*, has a shape as shown in Figure 5.2a.

Since we have argued that there exists a relationship between the level of excess demand for labour (which is not directly observable) and the rate of change of money wages, i.e. the reaction function, and a relationship between the level of the excess demand for labour and the level of unemployment, this should enable us to derive a relationship between unemployment and the rate of change of money wages. That is, we are using unemployment (an observable variable) as a proxy for excess demand for labour. However, now we make the 'jump' mentioned earlier and assume that the above relationships (for micro markets) are aggregated to give equivalent relationships at the macro level. With this in mind we now derive the aggregate relationship between the level of unemployment and the rate of change of money wages.

This derivation is illustrated in Figure 5.3. In quadrant (c) of Figure 5.3, the amount of unemployment is measured downwards on the vertical axis and the excess demand for labour, is measured leftwards on the horizontal axis. In this quadrant the relationship of Figure 5.2b is repeated. In quadrant (d) the hypothesised relationship between excess demand and the rate of change of money wages is shown. Finally, in quadrant (a) a relationship between the level of unemployment and the rate of change of money wages, labelled the 'Phillips curve', is drawn. This is the derived relationship between unemployment and the rate of change of money wages. How is this relationship obtained?

If we begin by assuming a level of unemployment of U_1 and then examine the excess demand–unemployment relationship in quadrant (c), we see that this level of unemployment implies an amount of excess demand for labour of E_{d1}. However, given our reaction function relating the rate of change of money wages to the level of excess demand for labour, which is plotted in quadrant (d), we see that this level of excess demand implies a rate of increase in money wages given by $\dot{W}_1$. (Note that for a representation of rates of wage changes, we are replacing $\Delta W/W$ with $\dot{W}$, i.e. a W with a dot above it.) All that remains to be done now is to transfer the level of unemployment from the downward vertical axis in quadrant (c) to the rightward horizontal axis in quadrant (b), and this gives us one point on the Phillips curve, namely, point A. The combination of variables at point A tells us that the unemployment level U_1 implies a rate of change of money wages of $\dot{W}_1$. Repeating this procedure for all levels of unemployment allows us to obtain a whole set of associated values for the rate of change of money wages. Joining these points gives the Phillips curve, which shows the rate of change of money wages associated with the various levels of unemployment.

It is important to remember that this relationship between the rate of change of money wages and the level of unemployment is a secondary or derived relationship. Its existence depends upon the two assumptions (1) that the rate of change of money wages is a positive function of the level of excess demand, and (2) that the level

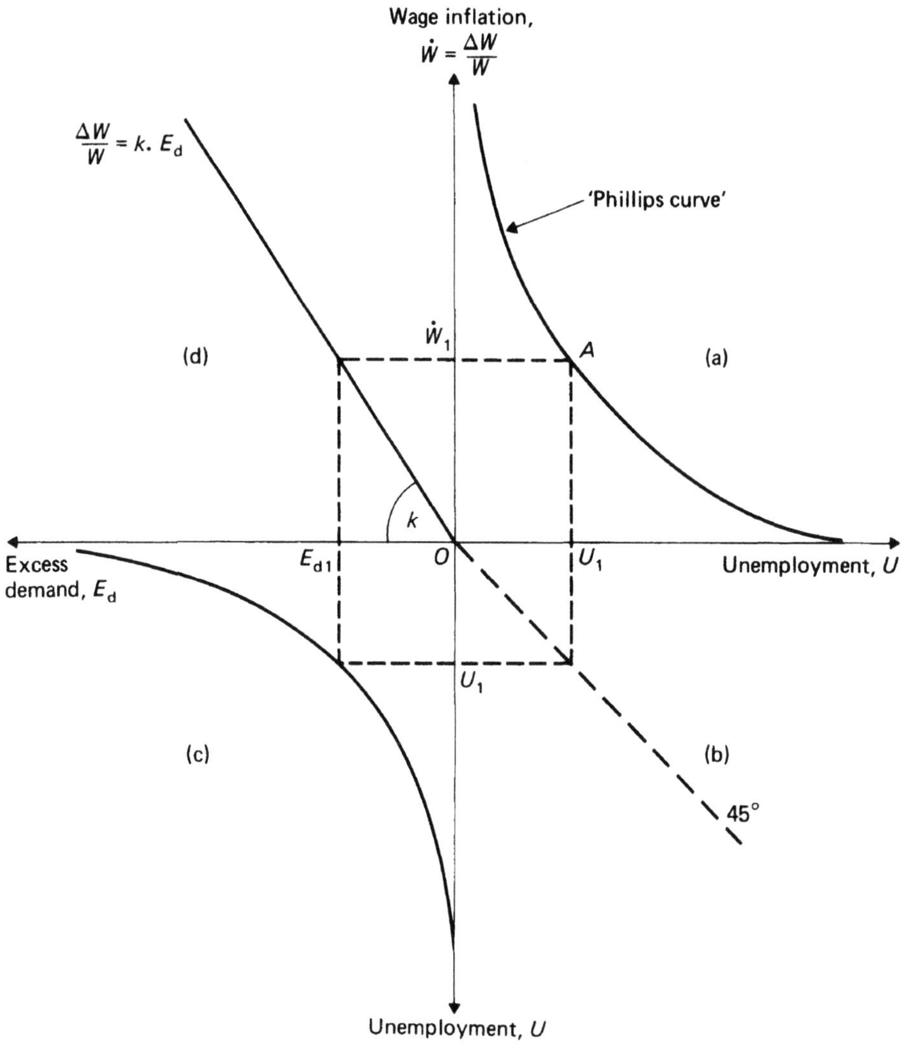

Figure 5.3 *One theoretical basis for the Phillips curve*

of excess demand is negatively related to the level of unemployment. However, the importance of the relationship is that it can be tested because it is between observable variables.

The seminal piece of work in the area was carried out by A. W. Phillips (1958). Using UK data for the years 1861–1957, he has shown that the average relation between unemployment and the rate of change of money wages was basically as shown in Figure 5.3, quadrant (a), i.e. that it was inverse, convex to the origin and had a positive intercept on the horizontal axis. Therefore, the lower the level of unemployment, the greater is the rate of increase of wages, and as unemployment decreases, these decreases in unemployment are associated with greater and greater rates of increase of wages.

So far we have been examining an excess demand approach to wage inflation, and below we return to consider some qualifications of the approach just outlined. In the meantime, however, let us turn to an alternative hypothesis and discuss what Hansen (1970) calls 'spontaneous wage changes'.

The distinguishing feature of spontaneous wage changes is that they nearly always occur in an upward direction, even in the absence of any excess demand in the labour market. The notion of spontaneous wage changes can be shown with the aid of Figure 5.1b. When there is no spontaneous wage change, the reaction function is plotted in Figure 5.1b as line *aa*. The important point to note about *aa* is that it assumes that, in the presence of zero excess demand, the rate of change of money wages will be zero also. Line *bb*, on the other hand, shows the reaction function with the presence of spontaneous wage changes. At zero excess demand there is still a positive rate of change of money wages, given by W^*, and at any level of excess demand the rate of change of wages is greater than it would have been had there been no spontaneous wages changes. It should be clear from Figure 5.3 that spontaneous wage changes have the effect of shifting the Phillips curve upwards, i.e. of increasing the rate of change of wages at each unemployment level.

The question now arises about the causes of these changes in wage rates when excess demand is lacking. There are many varieties of explanation, but basically two schools of thought may be distinguished. One school stresses the importance of economic factors other than excess demand. The argument is that many labour markets are far from the competitive ideal and that this allows a wide degree of flexibility in wage determination. It is well known that in situations of bilateral monopoly, i.e. a market with monopoly on the demand side (employers' federation) and monopoly on the supply side (trade union), the equilibrium wage rate is not unambiguously determined. The determination of wage rates in such conditions depends, *inter alia*, on bargaining carried out between the parties. One argument holds that the determination showed in the bargaining of the supply side of the market is a function of the aggressiveness of trade unions. There is an obvious problem posed in trying to test this theory, namely, the obtaining of some index of union militancy. An index has been proposed by Hines (1964), who argues that a prerequisite for militancy in wage bargaining by the unions is that they recruit new members to their numbers. Hines has in fact found some empirical support for the proposition that the *rate of change* of the percentage of the labour force unionised, to be viewed as an index of militancy in the wage-bargaining procedure, has some effect on the rate of change of money wage rates.

The second approach to the explanation of spontaneous wage changes does not turn to such economic explanations; rather it argues that the causes are outside the realm of economic analysis and are mainly sociological in nature. There are many diverse schools which subscribe to such sociological explanations. Some see it as a reflection of the 'decadence' of modern society, so that we have one economist speaking of the causes of recent wage increases and stating that 'my own opinions are that the causes are sociological' and that 'all of this has been made possible, of course, by a certain permissiveness' (Harrod, 1972). Others subscribing to the sociological explanation argue that dissatisfactions over the prevailing distribution of income and wealth in the economy, together with the slow rate of economic growth of real income, have caused frustration among labour, leading to 'wage explosions'.

So far we have looked at the excess demand and spontaneous wage-change theories of wage inflation. The excess demand theory has been summarised by the Phillips curve. While we have shown that the concept of spontaneous wage changes can be analysed as an upward shift of the Phillips curve, there has, however, been a serious attack on the theory behind that relationship, which has important repercussions on any explanation of the rate of change of money wages. In Figure 5.2a we drew the demand and supply schedules of labour in terms of the *money* wage rate. However, the neoclassical theory of the labour market assumes that the demand and supply of labour depend upon the level of the *real* wage rate, i.e. money wages divided by some appropriate price index. The reasoning behind this should be fairly obvious, since it is the money wage rate *relative to the money value of what is being produced* that determines the profitability of hiring labour and the optimality of the work–leisure decision.

Since contracts to set money wage rates are struck at discrete intervals, typically annually, the effect of the above realisation is that expectations of price level changes must now enter as an independent factor affecting money wage changes. Therefore anticipations of price level changes will lead to increases in money wages independently of the state of excess demand.

Now it may be thought that expectations of price level changes can simply be added to the Phillips curve relation along with the notion of spontaneous wage changes to obtain the total change in money wages. However, some economists argue that, once anticipated price changes are added as a factor determining wage rate changes, the Phillips curve relation breaks down. This may be explained by the use of a simple model, as follows:

$$\dot{W}_t = f(U_t) + \alpha \dot{P}_{te} \quad (1)$$

$$\dot{P}_t = \dot{W}_t \quad (2)$$

$$\dot{P}_{te} = \dot{P}_{t-1} \quad (3)$$

Equation 1 indicates that the rate of change of money wages in time period t, $\dot{W}_t$, depends upon the level of unemployment in period t, U_t (i.e. on some form of the Phillips relation) and upon a proportion, α, of the expectations held in time period t of what the rate of price changes will be in the next time period, $\dot{P}_{te}$. Equation 2 illustrates the simple markup hypothesis that the rate of price inflation will be equal to the rate of wage inflation. It should be noted that equation 2 assumes that there is a total absence of productivity increases; if productivity were increasing, say at the rate of $\dot{M}_t$, then equation 2 would be of the form

$$\dot{P}_t = \dot{W}_t - \dot{M}_t$$

However, retaining equation 2 does not detract from the main argument. Equation 3 shows a very simple expectations-forming hypothesis. It states that expectations held in time period t of what the rate of change of prices will be in the following period is equal to the actual rate of change in prices in the period $(t-1)$.

The workings of the model are shown diagrammatically in Figure 5.4. In the diagram the rate of change of money wages, which by assumption equals the rate of change of prices, is measured up the vertical axis and the level of unemployment is measured along the right horizontal axis. The left horizontal axis also shows the rate of change of prices, which is reflected, through the 45° line, from the vertical axis. Consider the Phillips curve X_1X_1. (Since it makes no substantive difference to the argument that follows, but aids its exposition, the Phillips curve is assumed to be linear.) If the level of unemployment were U^* there would be neither wage nor price changes. However, suppose that the authorities, in time period 1, use some technique of demand management to reduce the level of unemployment from U^* to U_1. As a result, given the assumptions of the model, there will occur actual wage and price inflation of $\dot{W}_1 = \dot{P}_1$. This rate of inflation in period 1 is reflected on to the left horizontal axis as $O\dot{P}_1$. Consider now what happens in period 2. We assume that the authorities maintain the level of unemployment at U_1 in period 2, and that labour, bargaining for wages and employers paying them, introduce into their negotiations the factor of expectations. This 'price expectations' aspect of wage inflation is contained, as already mentioned, in equation 1 with the inclusion of the $\dot{P}_{te}$ term. However, according to equation 3, price expectations

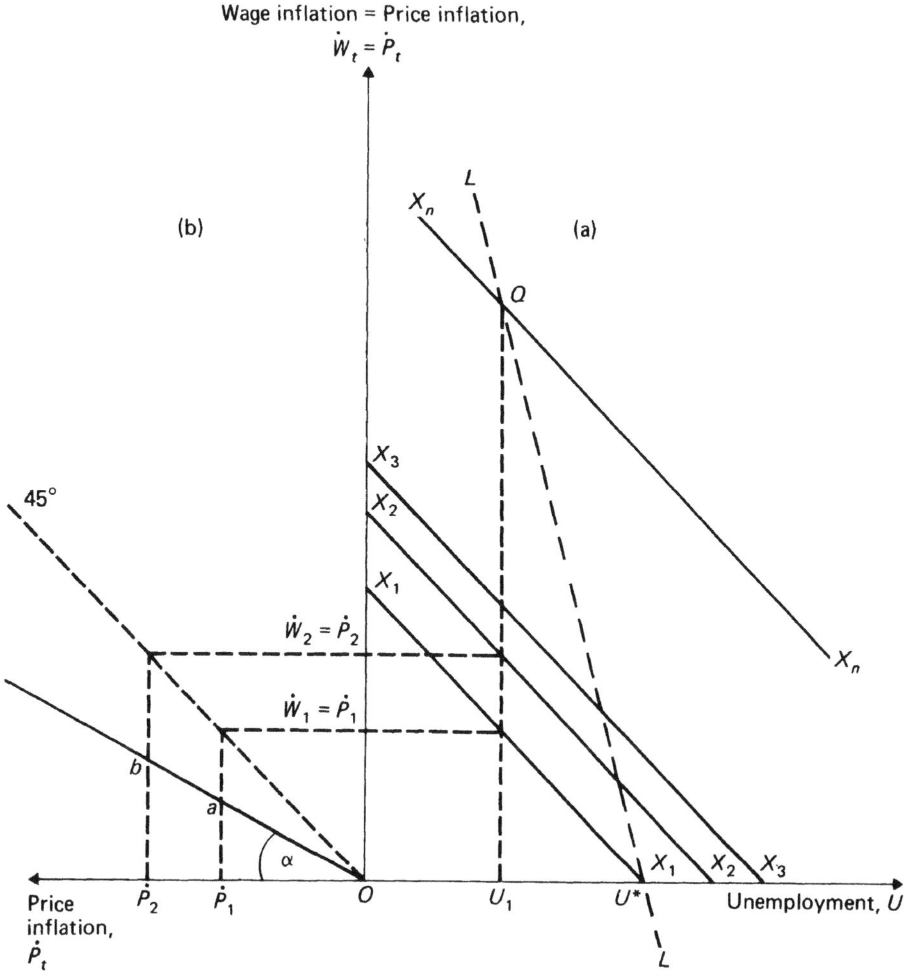

Figure 5.4 *Price expectations and inflation*

held in period 2 are equal to what the actual price inflation was in period 1. This actual inflation in period 1 is given by $O\dot{P}_1$, and a proportion, α, of this expectation is added to the 'basic' Phillips curve, $X_1 X_1$, (which shows rates of inflation and unemployment when there is no expected inflation) in order to determine wage inflation in period 2. Geometrically, this proportion, α, of $O\dot{P}_1$ is represented by the vertical distance $\dot{P}_1 a$ in quadrant (b) of the diagram, and this proportion is added to the 'basic' Phillips relation, $X_1 X_1$, to give $X_2 X_2$, which is the 'short run' Phillips curve relevant to period 2. Wage and price inflation in period 2, with unemployment held at U_1, is then $\dot{W}_2 = \dot{P}_2$. In time period 3 a proportion, α, of $O\dot{P}_2$, equal to $\dot{P}_2 b$, is added to $X_1 X_1$ to give $X_3 X_3$, and so on as before. We notice that as a result of introducing expectations of inflation the 'short run' Phillips curve moves upwards over time. However, as long as α is less than unity each upward movement is less than the previous one, and eventually the upward displacement approaches zero. This limiting position of the Phillips curve is given by $X_n X_n$. The long-run equilibrium rate of wage and price inflation corresponding to the level of unemployment U_1 is given by the vertical distance $U_1 Q$.

The above experiment could be repeated for each different level of unemployment other than U_1, and other points such as Q would be found showing the long-run equilibrium rate of wage and price inflation corresponding to each level of unemployment. The locus of such points is given in Figure 5.4 by line LL, and this is sometimes referred to as the long-run Phillips curve. It indicates that, when price expectations are introduced into the Phillips curve relation, the rate of inflations associated with any level of unemployment less than U^* is greater in the long run than in the short run.

An extreme view of the above expectations view of inflation is held by some economists (e.g. Friedman, 1968), who argue that the value of α in the model is unity. If this is so, it is easy to see that the short-run Phillips curve moves up by the amount $O\dot{P}_1$ each period, assuming an initial unemployment level of U_1 and that the rate of inflation does not converge to any long-run limiting value. This extreme view sees the long run trade-off as being a vertical line through the unemployment level U^*. Demand management policies designed to hold the level of unemployment below the level U^* imply an accelerating rate of inflation. Indeed only the level U^* is compatible with a constant rate of inflation; this level is referred to by Friedman as the 'natural rate of unemployment'.

Some of the tests of the expectations hypothesis (e.g. Solow, 1969) tend to discredit the extreme view of the hypothesis but do suggest that there is some validity in the notion, sufficient to give a more severe trade-off between unemployment and inflation in the long run than in the short run. On the other hand, some tests have found a value for the coefficient that is close to unity (e.g. Saunders and Nobay, 1972; Parkin, Sumner and Ward, 1974).

PRICES AND INCOMES POLICIES

Since the end of the Second World War the UK authorities, in attempting to curtail inflation, have instituted a wide variety of prices and incomes policies. These have ranged from voluntary policies, e.g. Cripps's wage standstill of 1948 and Brown's policy of voluntary restraint on prices and incomes (1964–6), through to policies that have had full statutory backing to fix pay and prices, e.g. the Labour government's period of controls (1966–9) and the Conservative government's policy of 1972–4. The policies have included 'freezes' on pay and prices (1966 and 1972), percentage norms (the 3 per cent 'norm' for wage increases of 1965) and absolute ceilings on wage increases (the £6 per week limit of 1975–6).

One feature of the use of prices and incomes policies in the United Kingdom is that, over the period since 1948, the policies themselves and the administration of the policies have become more complex. Cripps's policy was simple and straightforward, namely, that wages should rise in line with productivity. Later policies, however, were more complex as the loopholes and mistakes of previous policies became apparent. The increasingly complex policies called for more sophisticated machinery to administer them. For example, whereas Cripps's policy had no institution for its administration, the Labour government (1964–70) set up the National Board for Prices and Incomes to supervise its policies, and more recently the Conservative government's pay and prices policy was accompanied by two administrative bodies, namely, the Pay Board and the Price Commission.

In terms of the simple model of the inflationary process set out earlier, prices and incomes policies can be expected to operate in a variety of ways. This basic model indicated that excess demand, union pushfulness and price expectations will all lead to increases in wages, which, given productivity, in turn will lead to increases in labour costs per unit of output, and that firms, which are anxious to protect customary profit markups, will raise prices accordingly. Prices and incomes policies may operate on any or all of these channels.

INCOMES POLICY

In this section we examine how incomes policy may operate to curtail inflation and look at some of the difficulties that incomes policy faces. Later we turn our attention to prices policies.

Wage rises and excess demand

Incomes policy is an attempt by the authorities to set levels of wages independently of the levels that would be set by the participants of the wage bargain if these were left to themselves. The difficulties of implementing such a policy are at their greatest when there is excess demand in labour markets.

In Figure 5.5a, let the ray OX_1 represent the reaction function, linking the rate of change of money wages to the extent of excess demand when the authorities do not attempt to interfere via an

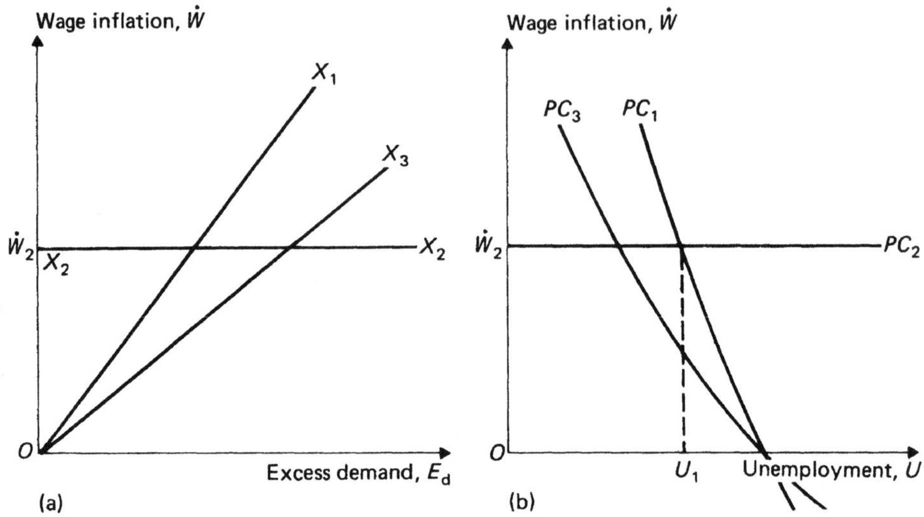

Figure 5.5 *Incomes policy and the Phillips curve*

incomes policy. Given the relationship between unemployment and excess demand shown in Figure 5.2b, we are also able to derive a Phillips curve corresponding to the reaction function OX_1. This is plotted as PC_1 in Figure 5.5b. Now the authorities may attempt to alter this situation in two different ways. First, they may attempt to circumvent market forces (summarised in the reaction function OX_1) entirely and impose a constant rate of change of wages. This decision is made irrespective of the state of excess demand in the market. This constant rate of change of wages may be induced by moral persuasion or by law, but whatever its basis the effect is to substitute the reaction function X_2X_2 for the original OX_1. The effect of such a policy is to cause the 'new' Phillips curve PC_2 (associated with the reaction function X_2X_2) to be horizontal at the level of the 'wage norm', $\dot{W}_2$. Alternatively, the authorities may try to retain some market forces but to weaken their strength. Therefore, this policy attempts to reduce the rate of change of money wages associated with any level of excess demand but does not try to replace market forces completely. The effect of this policy would be to flatten the reaction function, say to OX_3, and consequently the Phillips curve, say to PC_3.

Lipsey and Parkin (1970) have argued that incomes policy need not be an unmixed blessing. They have shown that at high levels of unemployment the effect of an incomes policy may lead to a higher inflation rate than would occur in its absence. This argument may be illustrated with the aid of Figure 5.5b. Suppose the authorities have substituted a fixed wage norm of $\dot{W}_2$, so that the Phillips curve is now PC_2 rather than PC_1. At levels of unemployment above U_1 the rate of inflation after the institution of the incomes policy would be above the rate that would exist in its absence.

We have already mentioned that a policy that tries to reduce or eradicate the effect of excess demand on wage rises is fraught with difficulties. What exactly are these difficulties? Paish (1968) argues that both employers and trade unions would face insuperable problems. On the employers' side, the fact that demand for labour exceeds the supply suggests that employers must have profitable orders that cannot be met because of the scarcity of labour. In such situations it is difficult to prevent employers from attempting to attract labour by offering higher wages. Equivalently, trade union leaders find it increasingly difficult to persuade their members to accept lower wage increases than the level that excess demand would dictate. Union leaders may be faced with the choice between allowing wages to rise and experiencing increasing dissatisfaction with their leadership among their rank and file.

It may be argued, of course, that these problems only apply if the policy attempted is one of persuasion. If the policy has the force of law behind it, how can even the imperatives of excess demand lead to its breakdown? The answer is that excess demand is like a fluid; if stopped from flowing down one channel, it will escape via another. The concept of the rate of change of wages is a fuzzy notion. Implicitly what we have been talking about is the wage rate, i.e. the rate of pay per hour. Suppose that a statutory policy is introduced which fixes wage rates. It is possible that, in situations of excess demand, the result of a policy that concentrates on controlling wage rates will be to raise wage costs through other channels. For example, employees might be regraded, thus putting them on a higher wage rate quite legally, with the result that unit labour costs and prices are raised. It is possible to envisage legislation which is more complex than legislation that merely prohibits any change in wage rates and which cuts out the specific loophole mentioned above. But all this more detailed legislation may only lead to more sophisticated ways of avoiding it, as well as spawning a bureaucracy to manage it. The conclusion then is that, in situations of excess demand for labour, incomes policy may not be too reliable for controlling wage costs to any great extent.

Some economists are even more pessimistic about the ability of incomes policies to come to grips with the problem of high inflation, arguing that they not only fail to improve the situation but may even make it worse. Suppose for the moment that an incomes policy is slightly successful in moderating the rate of change of wage increases; then it is argued that labour may react to this situation by attempting to find new and more highly paid jobs. That is, there occurs an increase in the amount of frictional unemployment. In terms of Figure 5.2a, the actual employment schedule, *EE*, moves to the left at all levels of the wage rate. This has the effect of raising the excess demand–unemployment mapping in Figure 5.2b; that is, any level of excess demand is now associated with a higher level of unemployment. If this effect is important enough to outweigh the moderating influence that incomes policy has had on the relation between excess demand and wage inflation (the reaction function), then it is possible that the Phillips curve will have moved upwards from its original position. This result is the opposite of the goal of an incomes policy. There is in fact some evidence that the relationship between excess demand and unemployment shifted in the United Kingdom in the late 1960s. Regarding whether this was caused by the application of incomes policy in this period, one survey of the problem (Bowers *et al.*, 1972) argues that there is 'some very tentative support for this hypothesis'.

Wage rises and trade union pushfulness

In the previous section we saw that in the presence of excess demand an incomes policy may not be successful in substantially altering the Phillips curve trade-off. However, this does not exclude the possibility that an incomes policy may have success in moderating the other suggested causes of inflationary impulses. If the rate of change in money wages is to a large extent determined by the level of union militancy or pushfulness, an incomes policy may have a role to play as an anti-inflationary device.

'Incomes policy' is a term that has different meanings for different people, but in respect of moderating union pushfulness two major kinds of policy have been advocated. First, some economists have applied the term 'incomes policy' to attempts to reduce or destroy the powers that unions have in wage bargaining. This type of policy tries to reduce the upward push on money wages caused by union militancy by an all-round reduction in the strength and power of unions. These policies might be analysed as basically being attempts to break up the monopoly power on the supply side of the labour market and to bring the labour market back to the 'ideal' of atomistic competition. It is argued that there are some simple institutional changes that would go a long way to introducing the above state of affairs. Examples such as the withdrawal of some of the legal privileges that unions enjoy and a reduction (or termination of) social security benefits to strikers' families are given. The major argument for this type of policy is that union pushfulness must be attacked at its source, any attempt at mere persuasion being useless. The views of Harberler (1972) are illustrative of this line of argument: 'The excessive power of labour unions should be curbed, there is simply no synthetic substitute for restoring a larger measure of competition in the labour market and elsewhere.' As previously mentioned, this type of policy is often referred to as incomes policy. However, we do not intend to use the term in that manner here. We shall consider that only the second type of policy, which aims to persuade unions to restrain the exercise of their power in wage bargaining, rightly belongs to the field of incomes policy. This is not to suggest that attempts to break up the sources of union power have not been made in the United Kingdom. It was such thinking that led to the Industrial Relations Act 1971 in which some strikes (nearly all unofficial strikes) were termed 'unfair industrial practices'. A National Industrial Relations Court was created which was entitled to call for a 'cooling off' period or a ballot of union members before a strike. This policy, however, is regarded here as lying in the field of industrial relations rather than incomes policy as such.

The second type of policy to deal with trade union pushfulness is that in which unions are persuaded to adopt less aggressive stances over wage bargaining and to accept the wage norms and restraints set by the government. This type of policy, unlike the one mentioned above, is not a call for a return to the workings of competitive markets; rather it argues that, since labour markets are not perfect, the wage-bargaining situation should be replaced by one in which the government becomes the agency that determines wage levels. Critics of incomes policies ask how a system of wage norms and persuasion could cause unions to demand wage rises below those which they could achieve by using their power. Johnson (1972) argues that it is a 'naïve proposal' to hope that unions will stop their wage push by 'appealing to the pushers' sense of decency'. Of course, if this type of policy comprised only an appeal to decency, it could not be expected to have much success. Obviously, the policy must involve some element that makes it in the unions' interest to moderate their pushfulness.

There are several possibilities here. One explanation of the cause of union pushfulness, which was mentioned earlier, is sociological in nature, i.e. dissatisfaction with the distribution of income in society. If this is in fact the case, an incomes policy that involved government intervention into the area of income distribution as well as into the area of income totals might stand more chance of success. The policy here is intended to mitigate the frustrations felt by various groups, which are a source of inflationary impulses in the economy.

It is true, of course, that any incomes policy has income distribution implications. What is meant here, however, is that in order to 'buy' acceptance of its wages policy the authorities take extra steps to change the distribution of income. Of recent interest is the so-called 'social contract'. This was an accommodation reached by the Labour Government and the trades unions in 1974. The government part of the deal was that they were to carry out social and industrial policies that were viewed favourably by the unions, e.g. higher pensions and social security payments, proposed wealth taxes and the repeal of the Industrial Relations Act 1971. The unions' part of the bargain was to moderate their wage claims. The wage guidelines formulated by the Trades Union Congress in June 1974 were that wage agreements should maintain real incomes, i.e. that wage increases should only keep up with price increases.

Wage rises and price expectations

It was shown earlier with the aid of Figure 5.4 that, if the authorities manage to lower the expected rate of inflation, this will 'improve' the trade-off between unemployment and inflation with which the policy maker is faced; that is, any given level of unemployment will be associated with a lower rate of inflation. Before discussing how income policies may achieve this, we must make a brief excursion into the problem area of how expectations are formed. Numerous hypotheses have been put forward, but the one most widely used in both empirical and theoretical work is that which suggests that current expectations of inflation are a *weighted average* of past values of inflation, with the most recent observations being given the heaviest weighting. In the model illustrated in Figure 5.4, the expectations hypothesis there used was an extreme case of the above, namely, that only the last period's inflation rate dictated expectations.

If it is in fact the case that current inflationary expectations are generated solely by past levels of actual inflation, then the potential effectiveness of incomes policy in affecting inflationary expectations is extremely slight. However, it is unreasonable to suppose that economic units form their expectations of the future value of a variable only by observing past values of the same variable. Presumably economic units will be willing to incorporate currently available information that is independent of past inflation rates into their forecasts of future inflation rates. For example, it is difficult to believe that the expectations of inflation were unchanged immediately after the miners' pay settlement of 1974, well before this pay rise started to affect actual prices. This being the case, there may indeed be a role for incomes policies in lowering inflationary expectations. They may serve as signals to the economy of the authorities' willingness and ability to reduce the rate of inflation, and they may also serve as a warning that past evidence of inflation is no longer a reliable guide as to what future rates of inflation are likely to be. However, as Laidler (1971) has pointed out, there is no *a priori* reason to believe that an incomes policy will be more successful in damping inflationary expectations if that success relies on an 'announcement' effect, than any other policy in which economic units have faith. In other words, any policy is likely to work if individuals believe that it will work. Therefore an announcement that a very tight monetary policy is to be introduced to curtail inflation is just as likely to have success as an incomes policy, if people have faith in that policy.

As an alternative to lowering inflationary expectations, a useful policy may be to stop economic units from incorporating into their wage bargains any expectations of inflation that they hold. One way of doing this is to promise units that if inflation actually takes place in future periods they will be compensated for it. Under this scheme, expected inflation ceases to be an independent factor causing inflation, since labour will have no reason to incorporate price expectations into their wage demands, because any actual inflation in future periods will give rise to wage increases.

A mild form of such 'wage indexation' was incorporated under the Stage Three of the Conservative government's incomes policy in 1973. Under this scheme, incomes were raised by 40p per week for every 1 per cent rise in the retail price index, above 6 per cent from its October 1973 level. Since in the years 1971–3 price inflation had been at an average annual rate of approximately 8·5 per cent, the policy was clearly designed to dampen down the effect that this high rate of price inflation would have, via inflationary expectations, on future wage demands.

The policy of wage indexation, while helpful under certain conditions and particularly when factors are causing inflation to slow down, can create problems. The compensation of incomes for price increases automatically ensures that real incomes cannot fall. This obviously creates problems in circumstances that call for a fall in real incomes. For example, the world commodity price rise, starting in 1972 and culminating in the quadrupling of oil prices in 1973–4, called upon real incomes in the United Kingdom to fall in this period. However, the automatic indexation of incomes to price rises exacerbated the situation. The authorities were certainly unpleasantly surprised to see, in early 1974, how quickly imported price increases were reflected in wage increases; see Miller (1976) on this point.

PRICES POLICY

The likely effectiveness of any government policy attempting to intervene directly in the price-setting process depends to a large extent on the price-setting hypothesis assumed. In general it may be said that adoption of the full cost plus markup hypothesis leaves little room for the success of a prices policy. The reason is that, in such a situation, a prices policy amounts to an attempt to hold price increases below the amount necessary to cover any cost increases. This of course reduces profits, and if continued indefinitely it must lead to negative profits, which is clearly an untenable position. The only role that prices policy can hope to play in this situation is to have a once-and-for-all effect of setting new profit margins; it cannot hope to continuously reduce them.

Price controls have been an important part of post-1972 government counter-inflation policy. These controls are embodied in a 'price code' administered by a Price Commission. While the provisions of the code have been subject to change, the major principle behind the operation of the scheme has been to limit the extent to which prices may be increased to changes in 'allowable' costs. What exactly has been 'allowable' has varied. For example, in the Conservative government's Stage Two, 'allowable' costs included only one-half of any increase in labour costs; this was later relaxed to 80 per cent of increases in labour costs in 1974. The obvious result of such policies is of course to squeeze profits, and there is some evidence that this in fact has occurred. (See Flemming, 1976.) Whether the squeeze on profits has been a contributory factor to the reduction in investment and the increase in unemployment over the period since 1972 cannot be dealt with here, but these potential and unpleasant side effects of price controls should be mentioned.

If, on the other hand, the level of excess demand is an important factor determining the setting of prices, then a prices policy may have some success in curtailing price increases. Analogous to a wages policy in the presence of excess demand, a prices policy may attempt (1) either completely to break the relation between excess demand and price increases by setting a price 'norm', or (2) to weaken the relationship. Equally so, a prices policy runs into the same difficulties as does a wages policy. Suppose, for example, that in a certain supply and demand situation a firm finds that its interests would best be served by raising its prices by 10 per cent but that (because of controls, guideposts or whatever) it feels constrained from doing so. Since the firm is constrained from profit maximising by changing one variable, namely, price, it will look for other variables which it can change to bring about the same result. An alternative variable is quality. The firm may well debase its product up to the point where the fixed original price amounts to the profit-maximising price on the now debased product. Whether this 'suppressed inflation' is as troublesome as 'open inflation' is an arguable point, yet it is hardly believable that the authorities impose price controls to create quality debasement of products. However, this may be one possible outcome of a prices policy.

MACHINERY OF PRICES AND INCOMES POLICIES

So far a simple model of the wage–price inflationary process has been outlined, and some of the various channels through which prices and incomes policies may enter that process to moderate the inflation rate have been looked at. We have also mentioned some of the specific problems that policy may come up against when it attempts to alter some of the variables that are considered to be important in the inflationary process. However, there are further factors which are important in determining the likely effectiveness of such policies.

An important point is that any policy must have, as a pre-requisite for its success, the consent of those economic units whose wages and prices it hopes to control. For this consent to be forth-coming at least two conditions must be met. First, the wage–price controls must be simple enough to be understood by all the parties concerned. Secondly, those parties concerned must regard the controls as being basically fair and equitable. To meet these twin goals of simplicity and equity, prices and incomes policies are often constructed in such a way as to have some fairly basic criteria for wage–price changes, while at the same time allowing a few exceptions to these criteria in the interests of flexibility.

What have been the usual criteria for allowing wage–price changes? We must distinguish between long run criteria and the criteria involved in special crisis circumstances – most usually balance-of-payments crises. However, we intend to concentrate on the former group. The most usual long-run criterion for allowing wage rises is that they should rise in line with the average productivity of labour. This, of course, implies that the basic rule for prices is that on average prices should not rise. This is so since wage rises, which are equal to the rate of increase of productivity, imply that on average unit labour costs are constant, which avoids any cost pressures on prices. Under the usual criteria, actual past increases in prices are not normally grounds for wage increases, because it is feared that to accept the principle that price rises constitute a valid criterion for wage rises would be to sanction explosive inflation; this is a fear of what is known as the wage–price spiral. This omission from the basic criteria for wage increases creates something of a problem. That is, if inflation is already under way and is proceeding at a rate greater than the rate of growth of productivity (to which wage increases are limited), this implies a fall in real wages.

While the basic criteria must be reasonably simple so that the policies can be easily understood, there must exist some means by which flexibility can be introduced into the policies to allow for consideration of equity and efficiency. On the grounds of equity, some UK policies since 1965 have permitted exceptions to the basic criteria in the cases of the 'low paid' and 'where there is widespread recognition that the pay of a certain group of workers has fallen seriously out of line with the level of remuneration for similar work' (Cmnd 2639, 1965). On the efficiency aspect, important exceptions to the basic criteria have been cases where productivity has risen due to labour changing their normal work practices (the so-called 'productivity bargain') and cases where in certain industries there have existed labour shortages requiring pay increases to alleviate them.

CONCLUSION: THE EFFECTIVENESS OF PRICES AND INCOMES POLICIES

Making an assessment of how effective prices and incomes policies have been in curtailing inflation involves a number of methodological problems. It is insufficient merely to compare the behaviour of prices and wages in periods when policies were operating with their behaviour in periods when policies were not operating. What is required is a comparison of how wages and prices did behave during periods when policies were operating with how they *would have behaved* if the policies had not been introduced. The correct approach, therefore, is to construct a model that explains the movements of wages and prices in terms of factors (other than prices and incomes policies), e.g. the level of unemployment, and then to use the model to predict what the behaviour of prices and wages would have been in the absence of prices and incomes policies. These predictions are then compared with the actual behaviour of prices and incomes, as modified by prices and incomes policies.

As presented above, the assessment of the effect of the policies appears straightforward. This is not so, however. For example, there is the difficulty of deciding where the line should be drawn between 'policy-on' and 'policy-off' periods. That is, should the end of the 'policy-on' periods be taken as those times when it has been officially announced that the operation of the policy has ceased? Or should the 'policy-on' periods be extended in order to 'capture' lagged effects of the policies? Furthermore, there is a problem in that UK prices and incomes policies have been so heterogeneous; they have ranged from statutory 'freezes' to calls for voluntary restraint. Yet in assessing the effectiveness of UK policies, this wide range of policies has been treated as if the policies have constituted a homogeneous variable. Bearing these difficulties in mind, we finally state some of the broad conclusions to which studies of the effectiveness of UK policies have come.

Most studies have concluded that UK prices and incomes policies have been relatively unsuccessful in curtailing wage and price inflation. The most successful periods have been those during which 'freezes' have been imposed on pay and prices. For example, it has been estimated that Cripps's (1948–50) policy lowered weekly wage rates by 2·5 percentage points below what they would otherwise have been. A Department of Employment Working Party (1971) estimated that the effect of the Labour government's mid-1960s policy was to keep the rise in earnings in the 1965–7 period 4 per cent below what it would otherwise have been, but to cause the rise in earnings in 1968–9 to be 4 per cent above what it would otherwise have been, giving an overall policy impact of nil.

We conclude with two quotes from a comprehensive assessment of postwar UK prices and incomes policies – quotes that are indicative of most other findings: 'incomes policy apparently has little effect either on the wage determination process or on the average rate of wage inflation'; and on prices, 'there is no evidence that incomes policy has produced a consistent change in the price equation' (Parkin, Jones and Sumner, 1972).

Chapter 6

Balance-of-payments Policy

In the discussion of policy objectives in the introductory chapter, where we examined the concept of the balance of payments and the distinction between current account and capital account transactions, the goal of balance-of-payments policy was taken as the elimination of a payments deficit or surplus on the official settlements definition. An adequate measure of the success or failure of policy would be provided by the balance-of-payments accounts, one of whose entries would be the amount of foreign exchange bought or sold by the official monetary authorities during the accounting period. However, these accounts are not particularly useful for policy formulation since they merely record the success or failure of past policy. What the policy maker wishes to know, as far as possible, is what the balance-of-payments position will be if certain policies are carried out. To examine this problem, the concept termed by Machlup (1950) as the 'market balance of payments' is the first thing to be looked at.

THE MARKET BALANCE OF PAYMENTS

The notion of market balance is concerned with the foreign exchange market, employing supply and demand schedules for foreign exchange. The supply of foreign exchange represents the sum of the supplies of foreigners who, wishing to purchase UK exports (the United Kingdom is taken here to represent the 'home' country) or make investments in or transfers to the United Kingdom, must supply foreign currency in exchange for sterling to enable them to carry out these transactions. Similarly, the demand for foreign exchange represents the sum of the demands of UK residents who wish to purchase imports, undertake foreign investments or make transfers abroad. Let us now examine the supply and demand for foreign exchange more closely.

The supply of foreign exchange

The market for foreign exchange consists of markets for the currencies of many economies. However, discussion here is restricted to the market for US dollars; that is, the dollar is used to represent

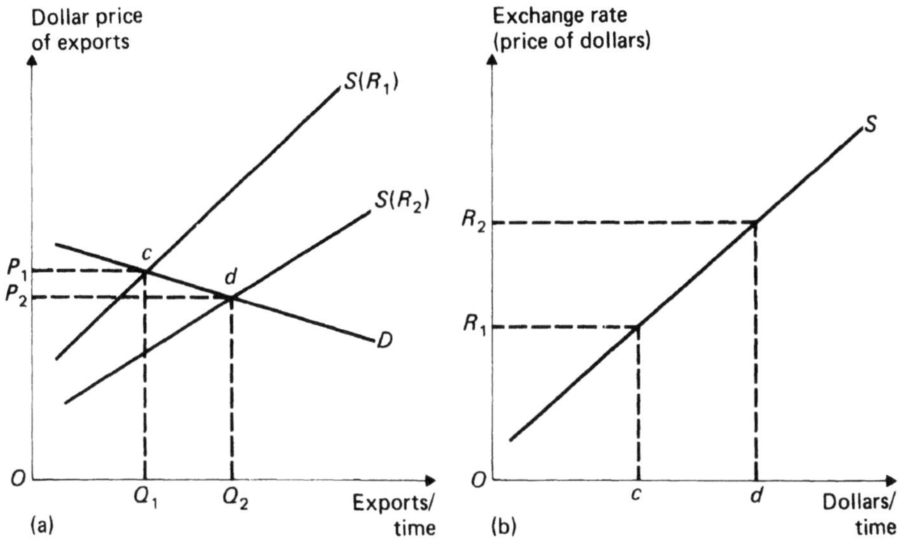

Figure 6.1 *The market for exports and the supply of dollars*

all foreign exchange. This simplification does not seriously affect the results of the following analysis, but it does aid its exposition.

The supply schedule of dollars shows the various quantities of dollars that would be supplied (in exchange for pounds) at each hypothetical rate of exchange. We select to look at the exchange rate in terms of the number of pounds required to purchase one dollar, i.e. the price of dollars in terms of pounds. Other factors apart from the exchange rate will affect the supply of dollars (e.g. domestic and foreign interest rates, price levels and levels of economic activity), but we employ the *ceteris paribus* assumption and hold these other factors constant for the moment.

It was mentioned above that one important source of the supply of foreign exchange was foreigners wishing to purchase UK exports. Let us examine this source more closely. In Figure 6.1a the demand and supply schedules for UK exports are represented. Note, however, that these relate the quantities of exports supplied and demanded to their *dollar price*. Supply curve $S(R_1)$ shows the supply of exports as a function of their dollar price, given exchange rate R_1. This schedule has a positive slope, reflecting the fact that, given the exchange rate, the higher the dollar price the greater also will be the sterling price and that the higher the sterling price the larger will be the quantity that producers are willing to supply. Consequently, quantity OQ_1 will be sold at price OP_1, and the quantity of dollars supplied for this purchase is given by area OP_1cQ_1. This therefore gives us one point on the supply curve of dollars, which is shown in Figure 6.1b. Given the exchange rate R_1, the quantity of dollars supplied at this rate is Oc, which is equal to area OP_1cQ_1 in Figure 6.1a.

Now assume that the exchange rate rises to R_2, i.e. that it requires a greater number of pounds to buy one dollar. This causes the supply curve of UK exports to move downwards to $S(R_2)$ (by the percentage of the exchange rate change). This is so since, following the exchange rate change (which is a depreciation of sterling), any dollar price now translates into a higher sterling price. Therefore the export producers, in order to receive the same amount of sterling from a given sale of exports as they received before the exchange rate change, now require to charge a lower dollar price. The new equilibrium in the market for UK exports is now at point d, giving a supply of dollars represented by area OP_2dQ_2. In Figure 6.1b this supply of dollars, at the new exchange rate R_2, is given by Od. However, there is no *a priori* reason for the supply of dollars at exchange rate R_2 to be greater than the supply when the rate was R_1. It will be greater if the price elasticity of demand for UK exports is greater than unity over the range under consideration. Furthermore, the larger is the price elasticity of demand for UK exports, the larger will be the increase in the quantity of dollars supplied as the result of a given depreciation of sterling. It is assumed here that the price elasticity of demand is greater than unity, and so the supply curve of dollars in Figure 6.1b is upward sloping.

What can be said about the supply of dollars to make investments in the United Kingdom? Leaving aside for the moment the problems of speculative transactions based upon anticipated changes in the exchange rate, capital flows will not be affected by the level of the exchange rate. Different exchange rates, as long as they remain unchanged, leave the rate of return on an investment unaltered. Therefore the supply of dollars to finance investment in the United Kingdom by foreigners will be inelastic when drawn against the exchange rate, and the total quantity of dollars supplied at each rate of exchange is given by schedule S in Figure 6.1b plus a given amount to finance investment in the United Kingdom.

The demand for foreign exchange

The demand for foreign exchange arises from UK imports and from UK residents wishing to make investments and transfers abroad. The demand schedule for foreign exchange relates the quantity of foreign exchange demanded at each level of the exchange rate, and its derivation is carried out similarly to that of the supply schedule for foreign exchange.

We begin by considering the market for UK imports, which is represented in Figure 6.2a. The demand and supply schedules in

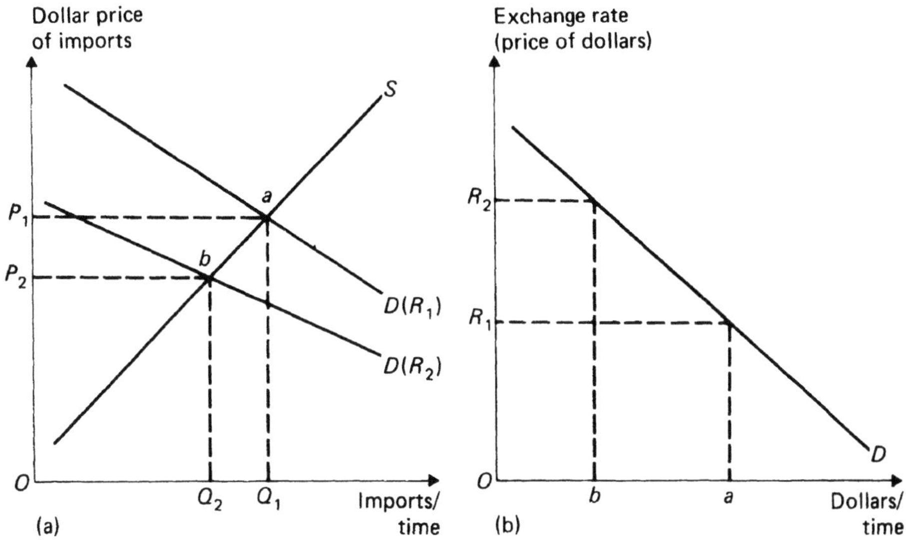

Figure 6.2 *The market for imports and the demand for dollars*

Figure 6.2a give the quantities of UK imports demanded and supplied as a function of their dollar price. Demand curve $D(R_1)$ shows the demand for imports, given exchange rate R_1. With the exchange rate at R_1 the quantity of imports purchased will be OQ_1 at price OP_1. Therefore the quantity of dollars demanded (to purchase quantity OQ_1 of imports), at exchange rate R_1, is given by area OP_1aQ_1. This gives us one point on the demand schedule for dollars as shown in Figure 6.2b; that is, at exchange rate R_1 the quantity of dollars demanded is Oa.

If the exchange rate rises to R_2, i.e. if a larger number of pounds is required to purchase one dollar, the demand schedule for imports moves downwards to $D(R_2)$ (by the percentage of the exchange rate change). This is so since, following the exchange rate change, any sterling price translates into a lower dollar price. The quantity of imports purchased will now be OQ_2 at a price OP_2. Therefore, with exchange rate R_2 the quantity of dollars demanded is given by area OP_2bQ_2. This gives us another point on the demand schedule for dollars in Figure 6.2b; namely, at exchange rate R_2 the quantity of dollars demanded is Ob.

The demand schedule for dollars in Figure 6.2b indicates that the higher is the price of dollars (in terms of pounds), the lower will be the quantity of them demanded. The reader may verify for himself that the more elastic is the demand curve for imports, the larger will be the reduction in the quantity of dollars demanded for a given rise in the exchange rate.

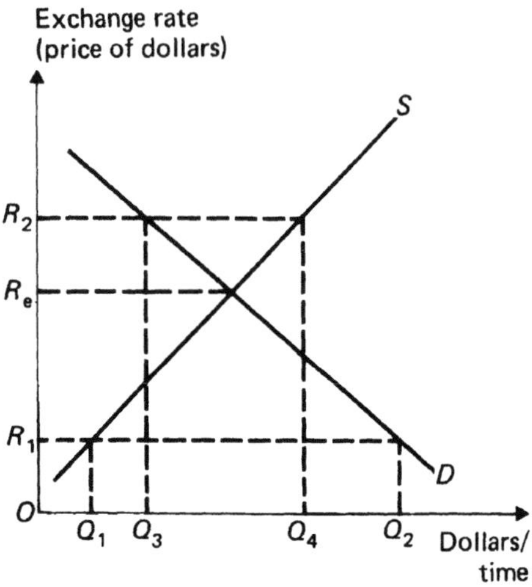

Figure 6.3 *The 'market balance of payments'*

As in the case of the supply of foreign exchange, if we leave aside for the moment the problems associated with speculative transactions based upon anticipated exchange rate changes, we can say that the demand for foreign exchange by UK residents wishing to undertake investments abroad will be unaffected by the level of the exchange rate. Therefore the total quantity of dollars demanded at each exchange rate is given by schedule *D* in Figure 6.2b plus a given amount to finance foreign investment.

The meaning of the 'market balance of payments' may now be illustrated with the aid of the demand and supply schedules of foreign exchange, as shown in Figure 6.3. Take, for example, the position when the exchange rate is given as R_1. At this rate, UK residents wish to demand quantity OQ_2 of dollars while foreigners wish to supply only quantity OQ_1; that is, at exchange rate R_1 there is a balance-of-payments deficit of $(OQ_2 - OQ_1)$. Similarly, if the exchange rate is at the level R_2 in Figure 6.3, there is an excess supply of dollars of the amount $(OQ_4 - OQ_3)$, which indicates a balance-of-payments surplus of that amount.

BALANCE-OF-PAYMENTS POLICIES

There are a number of policies which the authorities may undertake in the face of a balance-of-payments deficit. (In Chapter 1 we also saw why a persistent surplus may also be undesirable.) In the remaining sections of this chapter we consider some of the major policies that may be undertaken. The major policies to be considered are exchange rate changes, domestic deflation, the use of the differential between domestic and foreign interest rates in order to engineer a position on the capital account of the balance of payments that is similar in size (but opposite in sign) to the current account position, thereby giving overall balance-of-payments equilibrium, and, finally, direct controls on trade.

EXCHANGE RATE CHANGES

We saw above that at exchange rate R_1 in Figure 6.3 there existed a balance-of-payments deficit. This representation of the foreign exchange market implies that a rise in the level of the exchange rate to R_e will remove the deficit and bring about balance-of-payments equilibrium. There are, however, a number of exchange rate policies, in the sense that there are a number of exchange rate regimes within which the rate adjustment may be made.

Under a 'fixed exchange rate' system the authorities 'fix' the rate at some particular level. In fact the rate is allowed some freedom, namely, to move 1 per cent each side of its par value. If, for example, the authorities decide to maintain the rate at R_1 in Figure 6.3 (an overvalued rate for sterling), they may accommodate the resulting deficit, i.e. provide the excess quantity of dollars demanded and purchase the comcomitant excess supply of sterling, by running down their reserves and/or by borrowing from other international monetary authorities. (Alternatively, they may undertake policies to 'shift' the demand and supply schedules of foreign exchange so that they intersect at exchange rate R_1. For a discussion of these policies, see below.) However, if the authorities are convinced that the rate for sterling is overvalued because of some permanent structural shift, e.g. a permanent decrease in the demand for UK exports, they may decide to change the level at which they fix the rate. That is, they will devalue sterling, say to R_e, to remove the deficit. The United Kingdom operated such a system between 1945 and 1972, during which time two changes in the rate were made (in 1949 and 1967).

One alternative to the fixed rate system is for the authorities to allow the exchange rate to 'float'. In this case the authorities refrain from intervening in the foreign exchange market and allow the rate to be determined by market forces. Therefore, in terms of Figure 6.3, under a 'floating rate' system the existence of excess demand, as at R_1, would cause the rate to rise automatically towards the equilibrium level. In 1972 the UK authorities allowed sterling to float. However, the greater degree of flexibility implied by this policy change should not be interpreted as meaning that the exchange value of sterling, which would be dictated by the market, was no longer a matter of concern. The authorities have frequently intervened to prevent sharp fluctuations in the rate without attempting to prevent the long term depreciation of sterling that has occurred since 1972. The fixed rate and the floating rate systems should be regarded as the opposite extremes of a spectrum with other possible regimes, of varying degrees of flexibility, lying in between (e.g. the crawling peg system, in which adjustments are made to the par value of the currency more frequently than under the fixed rate system).

In a later section we consider some of the arguments that have been presented in favour of floating as opposed to fixed rates. In the meantime, however, we must examine more closely how and under what conditions an exchange rate change brings about a desired adjustment in the balance of payments. This examination is undertaken in the context of a depreciation of sterling to remove a UK deficit.

The effect that a sterling depreciation has in the markets for UK exports and imports is of crucial importance to the question of whether or not the sterling depreciation will remove a balance-of-payments deficit, i.e. an excess demand for foreign exchange. As we saw in Figure 6.1a, a sterling depreciation lowers the dollar price of UK exports, causing a larger quantity of them to be demanded. However, whether or not total dollar expenditure on UK exports increases or decreases as a result, depends on the price elasticity of demand for UK exports over the range under consideration. If demand is elastic, a larger quantity of dollars will be supplied to purchase the increased quantity of exports; if demand is inelastic, a smaller quantity of dollars will be supplied. In Figure 6.1a (and consequently in Figure 6.3) we assumed that the demand for UK exports is elastic. Note, however, that the upward-sloping supply curves in Figure 6.1a imply that UK exporters do not reduce the dollar price of exports by the full extent of the depreciation.

The effect of a sterling depreciation is to *raise the sterling* price of imports and (given an upward-sloping supply curve for imports) to *reduce the dollar* price of imports, as illustrated in Figure 6.2a. The upward-sloping supply curve of imports indicates that the sterling price of UK imports have not been raised by the full extent of the depreciation. Nevertheless, the sterling depreciation reduces the quantity of imports and the quantity of dollars demanded to purchase the reduced quantity of imports. Furthermore, the larger is the elasticity of demand for imports, the larger will be the reduction in the quantity of dollars demanded for any given depreciation of sterling.

It can be demonstrated that if the sum of the demand elasticities for exports and imports (assuming infinite supply elasticities) is greater than one, a sterling depreciation will improve the UK balance of payments.

A number of recent studies have attempted to measure the size of the price elasticities for UK exports and imports, the most comprehensive of which are perhaps those of the National Institute of Economic and Social Research (NIESR) (1972) and Artus (1975). Both of these studies were motivated by the desire to estimate the impact of the 1967 sterling devaluation on the UK balance of payments. One of the main problems in attempting a study such as the NIESR and Artus studies is that allowance must be made for factors, other than the exchange rate change, that will affect the balance-of-payments position. For example, the introduction of the import deposit scheme (November 1968) and a contraction of domestic demand had a favourable effect on the balance of payments, whereas the reduction in aid to exporters and the Kennedy Round of tariff reductions could be expected to work in the opposite direction. However, the NIESR study estimates that the export and import price elasticities were −1·4 and −0·25 respectively, and that by 1970 the devaluation had improved the balance of visible trade by £130 m. and the current account by £425 m. On the other hand, Artus, working at a less aggregated level, i.e. subdividing exports and imports into a larger number of classifications, obtains more optimistic results. He estimates that by 1970 the 1967 devaluation had improved the balance of trade by £726 m. and the current account by £1,036 m. In making these estimates, Artus calculates the export price elasticities for semi-finished manufactured goods and finished manufactured goods as −2·5 and −1·4 respectively and the import price elasticities for the same two groups of goods as −3·4 and −1·0 respectively. He takes estimates for the elasticities of exports and imports of fuel, food and raw materials from another study.

The aim of a sterling depreciation is to improve the UK balance of payments by changing the relative prices of UK and foreign-produced goods, thereby switching the demand of UK residents away from imports and towards domestically produced substitutes and the demand of foreigners towards UK goods. However, even if the values of the elasticities of demand for exports and imports are sufficiently large for such switching to occur, the exchange rate change does not need to be sufficient to ensure success in bringing about balance-of-payments adjustment. The switch in demand towards UK-produced goods requires a movement of resources into the industries producing exports and import substitutes. If the economy is operating close to full employment, the exchange rate change will require a contraction of domestic demand in order to 'free' resources to move into the industries producing exports and import substitutes. Otherwise the increased demand for the economy's full-employment output is likely to raise the domestic inflation rate, adversely affecting the competitive advantage that the depreciation originally gave to UK goods.

One of the assumptions under which the supply and demand schedules for foreign exchange in Figure 6.3 were drawn was that all other variables affecting the supply and demand for foreign exchange – other, that is, than the exchange rate – were held constant. Specifically, they were drawn under the assumption that domestic expenditure was fixed.

Total domestic expenditure, E, may be divided into residents' consumption expenditure, C, investment expenditure, I, and government expenditure, G. Parts of these components of total expenditure will be on imported goods, and it is likely that the higher is total expenditure, the higher will be the demand for imports at any given rate of exchange. Therefore there will be a different demand schedule for foreign exchange for different levels of domestic expenditure. This is shown in Figure 6.4a, where the demand schedules $D(E_1)$, $D(E_2)$ and $D(E_3)$ are those for successively higher levels of domestic expenditure. For the purposes we have in hand, it is useful to transfer on to a separate diagram the combinations of exchange rates and levels of domestic expenditure that give balance-of-payments equilibrium. Such a locus of combinations is given by line *BB* in Figure 6.4b. *BB* is positively sloped owing to the fact that an increase in domestic expenditure (from any point on *BB*), at an unchanged exchange rate, creates an excess demand for dollars, i.e. a balance-of-payments deficit. If this excess demand for dollars is to be removed, the exchange rate (price of dollars in terms of pounds) must rise. That is, positions below *BB* are combinations of exchange rates and levels of domestic expenditure that yield balance-of-payments deficits; the converse applies to positions above *BB*.

Also shown in Figure 6.4b is schedule *YY*. This is the locus of combinations of exchange rates and levels of domestic expenditure that maintain full-employment output. How can the negative slope of this schedule be rationalised? The level of domestic output, Y, equals the sum of the various categories of expenditure comprising it. In conventional national-income accounting, it is depicted as the sum of total expenditure by residents, $(C+I+G)$, minus the expenditure of residents that goes on imports, M, plus the expenditure by foreigners on domestic output (i.e. exports), X. Therefore output is given as

$$Y = C+I+G+(X-M)$$

where $(X-M)$ is the trade balance. Suppose that the levels of domestic expenditure $(C+I+G)$ and of the trade balance are just suf-

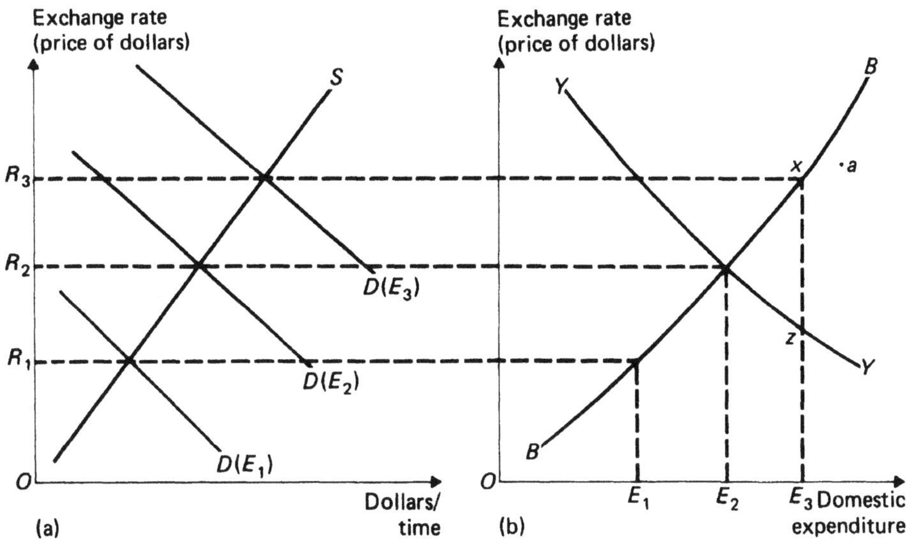

Figure 6.4 *Internal and external equilibrium*

ficient to purchase the full-employment level of output. If domestic expenditure is increased, the trade balance must be reduced if total demand is not to outstrip the full-employment level of output. Although the increased expenditure itself will increase imports and go some way towards reducing the trade balance, unless all of the increased expenditure goes on imports the rest of the reduction in the trade balance will have to come about by a change in the exchange rate. This requires a fall in the exchange rate (a fall in the price of dollars), which reduces expenditures on UK exports and increases those on UK imports. Therefore *YY* is negatively sloped in Figure 6.4b, and points above *YY* represent situations in which there is demand in excess of that required to purchase full-employment output; the converse applies to points below *YY*.

In Figure 6.4b there is only one combination of the exchange rate and the level of domestic expenditure that yields both balance-of-payments equilibrium and equality between full-employment output and total demand for that output; this combination is given by R_2 and E_2.

Important policy implications may be illustrated by reference to Figure 6.4b. First, correct policy responses are often counter-intuitive. Consider, for example, the position represented by point *a* in Figure 6.4b, which corresponds to a balance-of-payments deficit and a situation of excess demand for full-employment output. The deficit might indicate a rise in the exchange rate (a devaluation of sterling). However, it must be considered that domestic expenditure also would have to be reduced; this would lead to a balance-of-payments surplus, which would call for a revaluation of sterling.

A further implication is that a policy that relies purely on the exchange to affect the balance of payments, without control over domestic expenditure, is unlikely to be successful. For example, imagine that the economy is at a position represented by point *z* in Figure 6.4b; that is, it has a deficit on the balance of payments but a full-employment level of output. It might be attempted to cure the balance-of-payments position by a depreciation of the exchange rate, keeping the level of domestic expenditure constant at E_3, i.e. by a move to point *x* on *BB*. However, at point *x* there is excess demand for full-employment output. This is so since, whereas domestic expenditure has remained constant, the other component of demand namely, the trade balance, has been increased as a result of the exchange rate change. Consequently, the economy has been moved into an inflationary situation – an inflation that causes the improved trade balance to deteriorate again. Correct policy at point *z* would dictate not only raising the exchange rate to R_2 but also reducing domestic expenditure to E_2. This reduction in domestic expenditure releases resources, which are then available for use in the export and import substitution sectors, and consequently allows the expansion of output in these sectors without its resulting in inflationary pressure.

Bearing this in mind, it should not be too surprising that the sterling devaluation of 14·3 per cent in 1967 (a period when the UK economy was close to full employment) was coupled with a package of expenditure-reducing policies which included cuts in planned government expenditures, hire purchase restrictions and a ceiling on bank lending. While the direction of policy was correct, doubts soon began to arise about its magnitude. Although exports were rising, imports reacted sluggishly, and as this disappointing evidence accumulated during 1968, further expenditure-reducing policies were initiated, namely, large tax increases in the 1968 budget and further lending restrictions imposed on the banks. When these heavier expenditure-reducing policies were used the results of the devaluation were more gratifying; a current account deficit in 1968 of £270 m. was transformed into a surplus in 1969 of £460 m.

FIXED VERSUS FLOATING EXCHANGE-RATE REGIMES

In the previous section brief reference was made to the fact that exchange rate changes may be made within different types of exchange rate regimes. Two alternatives were outlined there, namely, a fixed rate regime and one in which the rate is left to float freely. It was also mentioned that there are intermediate regimes with varying degrees of flexibility. The choice of exchange rate regime is a matter of controversy among economists, and in this section we look at some of the relative merits of freely floating and fixed exchange-rate regimes.

The case for floating rates rests to a large extent on the continuous adjustment that they allow to changing conditions, e.g. changes in comparative advantages and in the relative rates of inflation between countries. They also reduce the need for countries to hold reserves, since, if the levels of exchange rates are to be determined freely on the foreign exchange market, no intervention by central authorities will be required to 'fix' rates at particular levels. However, from the point of view of domestic economic management, the importance of a floating rate system is that it removes the balance-of-payments constraint on the achievement of the full-employment objective; in short, it provides the authorities with an additional instrument of policy in their attempt to achieve simultaneously the objectives of macroeconomic policy (see Chapter 7).

This is not to suggest that balance-of-payments problems disappear if a floating exchange-rate system is adopted; they merely present themselves in different ways.

'Developments that would lead to a loss of reserves with a fixed exchange rate lead to a depreciation in the foreign exchange value of the currency if the exchange rate is allowed to float. In the first case, the loss of reserves will result, unless it is a once and for all loss, in a policy-induced contraction in domestic income while with a floating rate, the loss in real domestic purchasing power occurs automatically as import prices rise with the currency depreciation.' (Metcalfe, 1976)

One area of debate between those who support and those who oppose freely floating rates is concerned with the effect of speculators in a 'free' foreign exchange market. Supporters of floating rates tend to believe that the actions of speculators stabilise the exchange rate. For this to be so there must be a consensus among speculators about what the 'correct' rate should be, so that they purchase the currency when its price is 'too low' and sell it when its price is 'too high'. If this is the case, it is tantamount to the speculators taking over the role that the authorities play in maintaining a rate under a system of fixed rates. Opponents of floating rates, on the other hand, take a less optimistic view of the ability of speculators to know what the 'correct' rate is. Their view is that so much uncertainty abounds about the level of the 'correct' rate that the actions of speculators are likely to create substantial instability in the movements of exchange rates. For example, a fall in the exchange rate below the 'correct' level (about which speculators are uncertain) may lead speculators to extrapolate this movement and to sell the currency rather than buy it, which would be required if stability was to occur. Furthermore, it is feared that the instability in exchange rates caused by speculation has a detrimental effect on the volume of trade, because traders are discouraged by uncertainty about what the future levels of the exchange rate will be. However, this is a rather weak criticism, since there exist forward markets in which traders can contract to buy or sell foreign exchange some time in the future at an exchange rate that is currently known.

A futher argument of the opponents of floating rates concerns the effect that a depreciation of the domestic currency will have on the domestic price level of the country concerned. The fear is that a depreciation (by raising the domestic prices of imports) will raise industrial costs both directly (through higher raw material prices) and indirectly (through demands for higher wages) and that this will nullify the effect of the original depreciation, requiring a further depreciation. However, there are two points here. First, there is the question of whether or not, for most trading countries, imports bulk large enough for the effect on the domestic price level to offset completely the competitive advantage that the depreciation will have given to domestic producers. Secondly, those who favour excess demand explanations of inflation (see Chapter 5) see the line of causation running from domestic inflation to changes in the exchange rate. That is, if the UK inflation rate is higher than the inflation rates of the countries with which it trades, the exchange value of sterling will be falling on the foreign exchange market.

In 1972, at a time when the UK authorities expanded domestic demand in a 'dash for growth' policy, sterling was allowed to float in an attempt to remove the balance-of-payments constraint on faster growth. One month after the decision to float was taken, *The Economist* newspaper stated that 'Britain would probably break through to something like an economic miracle'. Yet, although by the end of 1975 sterling had depreciated by 30 per cent (against a weighted average of other major currencies) from its December 1971 level, the years since the float (particularly 1973–4) witnessed large deficits in the balance of trade and current account. Although these years coincided with a boom in world commodity prices and although in 1974 the price of oil was sharply increased, large capital inflows in 1974–5 (both private and official borrowings) would have been sufficient to insulate the exchange rate and the reserves if one other important factor had not been present, namely, the high rate of UK inflation relative to that of other countries. Since 1975 the position has improved, due to the curtailment of import growth as a result of the UK recession and as the effects of higher import prices have caused a switching in demand to UK-produced substitutes. Export demand has increased, due to increased price competitiveness as the exchange rate has continued to fall and as other industrialised countries have expanded their economies.

We have seen how exchange rate changes, by causing changes in the relative prices of UK and foreign-produced goods, bring about balance-of-payments adjustment. However, some economists (e.g. Thirlwall, 1974a) see the fundamental problem of the UK balance of payments as lying, not in its lack of price competitiveness in the goods that it exports, but in that it exports the 'wrong' kind of goods for world markets. A study by Houthakker and Magee (1969) estimates that the *income* elasticity of demand for UK imports is 1·7 and the *income* elasticity of demand of the rest of the world for UK exports is 0·9. These results indicate that, if the United Kingdom wishes to maintain a given exchange rate, it can only afford to grow half as fast as the rest of the world. Furthermore, a lowering of the exchange rate only changes the *levels* of exports and imports; it will not necessarily alter the rates of growth of exports and imports, unless the rate is allowed to depreciate continuously. Thirlwall is then led to suggest that, in the longer term, structural changes are required in the UK exporting sector whereby there is a switch in emphasis to the production and export of goods that have a high income elasticity of demand on world markets.

We now turn to consider why some countries may be loath to use exchange rate changes as a way of affecting the balance of payments. In terms of economic costs, there are at least two major reasons why exchange rate changes may be undesirable.

TERMS-OF-TRADE CHANGES

The terms of trade are defined as the exchange ratio between foreign and domestic goods and services. There are several alternative measures of this concept, but the one used here is the *net barter* terms of trade and is given as the ratio of the price of exports to the price of imports, i.e. P_x/P_m. The main significance of the terms-of-trade concept is in an examination of terms-of-trade changes over time (similar, for example, to the concept of the value of money). The terms of trade improve if the above ratio rises, since this allows the United Kingdom to purchase a larger quantity of imports for a given quantity of exports; the converse applies if a fall in the ratio occurs.

It is extremely important to stress that, when considering the terms of trade, the prices of exports and imports must be stated in the same currency. Failure to do this can lead to incorrect conclusions. For example, it is often said that a sterling depreciation

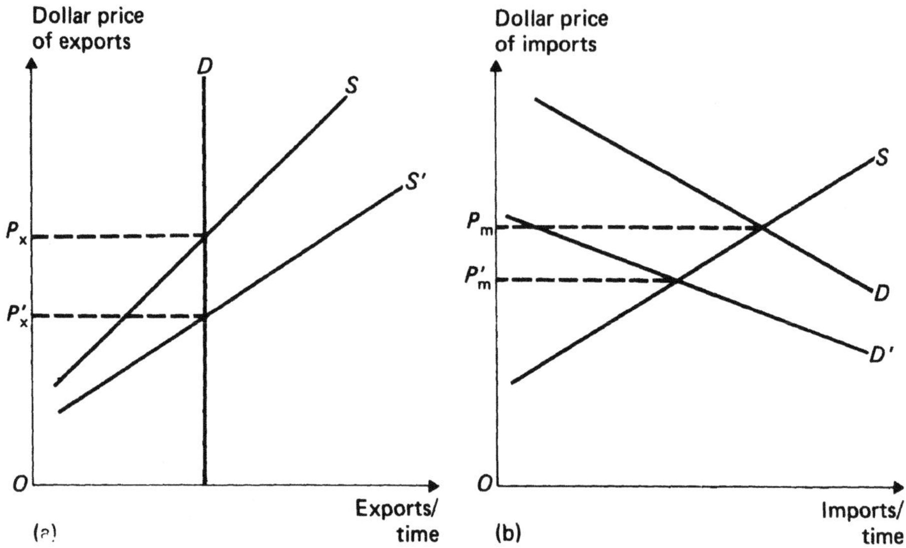

Figure 6.5 *The effect of a sterling depreciation on the United Kingdom's terms of trade – one possibility*

must worsen the United Kingdom's terms of trade because it 'cheapens' exports and makes imports more 'expensive'. But imports rise in *sterling* prices whereas exports fall in *dollar* prices. Here, as we have done up to now, we express their prices in a common currency, namely, the dollar.

The effect of exchange rate changes on the terms of trade depends upon the relative magnitudes of the supply and demand elasticities for exports and imports. As a general rule, a depreciation of sterling will worsen the UK terms of trade if the product of the supply elasticities is greater than the product of the demand elasticities. A proof of this assertion is beyond the scope of this book, and we merely illustrate one case in which the supplies of exports and imports are elastic, the demand for exports is completely inelastic and the demand for imports is elastic.

Figures 6.5a and 6.5b show the demand and supply schedules for exports and imports respectively. Note again that the quantities of exports and imports demanded and supplied are functions of their dollar prices. The original prices of exports and imports are given by P_x and P_m respectively. Consider now a depreciation of the domestic currency (sterling). The supply schedule of exports moves downwards (by the percentage of the depreciation) to S', lowering the price of exports to P'_x; that is, the price of exports falls by the full percentage of the depreciation since the demand is totally inelastic. The depreciation also causes the demand schedule for imports to shift downwards (by the percentage of the depreciation), lowering the price of imports to P'_m. However, in this case the price of imports does not fall by the full percentage of the depreciation. Therefore, since the price of exports has fallen by a larger percentage than that of imports, the effect of the depreciation has been to cause a deterioration in the terms of trade. It must be remembered that there are other configurations of demand and supply elasticities that would give the opposite result. The most that can be said is that it is possible for the use of the exchange rate as a balance-of-payments policy to imply an adverse movement in the terms of trade, but this is by no means a certainty. The question is basically an empirical one.

EXCHANGE RATE CHANGES AND AN INTERNATIONAL BANKING ROLE

Certain economic units in the world economy wish to hold foreign monetary assets. For example, there are various national monetary authorities which wish to hold such assets as part of their reserves.

The fact that sterling forms part of these international monetary assets held by foreign economic units entails benefits for the United Kingdom. These benefits occur because foreign units acquire the monetary claims on the United Kingdom in exchange for either goods and services or interest-yielding foreign securities. The sizes of these gains from being one of the issuers of the world's money can be large.

How might exchange rate changes affect the possibility of exploiting the above gains? They would affect them essentially by making foreigners less eager to hold UK monetary liabilities, i.e. less willing to give up resources to obtain them. Frequent exchange rate changes will cause greater uncertainty to surround the extent to which foreigners can hope for the value of their sterling assets to remain intact. Therefore the use of the exchange rate as an instrument of policy is likely to lead to a fall in the demand by foreigners to hold sterling balances, because sterling will have lost part of its attractiveness as money due to the greater uncertainty surrounding its value.

During the years prior to 1967, the UK balance-of-payments difficulties were exacerbated by withdrawals of foreign holdings of sterling, caused in the main by fears of the pound being devalued. Following the devaluation in 1967, many foreign holders attempted to run down their holdings of sterling. To counter this threat the so-called Basle facility was arranged, the main provision of which was that foreign official holders of sterling agreed to minimum holdings of sterling in exchange for a UK agreement to maintain the dollar value of such holdings.

If the authorities decide, for one reason or another, that they do not wish to reduce the foreign exchange value of the domestic currency in an attempt to remove a balance-of-payments deficit – i.e. that they wish to maintain an overvalued rate, as at R_1 in Figure 6.3 – there are a number of other policies that may be undertaken which reduce the demand for foreign exchange (shift the demand schedule in Figure 6.3 to the left) or increase the supply of foreign exchange (shift the supply schedule to the right). The remaining sections of this chapter are concerned with some of these policies.

DOMESTIC DEFLATION

We saw earlier that the higher is the level of domestic expenditure ($C+I+G$), the higher will be the demand for imports (and for foreign exchange) at any given level of the exchange rate. The discussion then was concerned with the need for domestic deflation to accompany an exchange rate depreciation, if the economy is close to full employment, in order that the competitive advantage given to exports should not be whittled away by the ensuing inflation. However, domestic deflation alone can be expected to improve the balance of payments, for a number of reasons. First, as already mentioned, a lowering of domestic expenditure will directly reduce the demand for imports. Secondly, if the lowering of domestic demand has the effect of reducing domestic costs and prices (or, at least, reducing their rate of increase), this may cause a switch in the demands of UK residents away from imports towards domestically produced substitutes and in the demands of foreigners towards UK exports.

Successive UK governments in the postwar period have contracted domestic demand, by imposing hire purchase restrictions, raising taxes and imposing controls on bank lending, in order to protect the exchange value of sterling. A major cost of demand contraction as a balance-of-payments policy is the higher level of unemployment that results. Furthermore, it has been argued that the frequent use of this policy in the United Kingdom adversely affected the economy's long-run growth rate in that business became more uncertain about future prospects and that industrial investment was lower as a result.

MONETARY–FISCAL POLICY MIX

The effectiveness of exchange rate variation in improving the balance of payments was shown to lie in the impact that it had on the current account. Mundell (1962), however, has pointed out that, since the balance of payments comprises transactions on both current and capital accounts, with an appropriate mix of monetary and fiscal policy the goals of balance-of-payments equilibrium and internal balance may be jointly attained.

It is argued that the current account is to a large extent determined by domestic expenditure and by the level of the exchange rate (it is also affected by the level of demand in the rest of the world) but that capital account transactions are determined by the differential between domestic and foreign interest rates. Furthermore, it is argued that any given level of domestic expenditure is compatible with any given level of the domestic interest rate by a suitable combination of monetary and fiscal policy. Therefore the capital account of the balance of payments can be set at the level of, but opposite in sign to, the current account by the requisite choice of monetary and fiscal policy. As an illustration, refer back to Figure 6.4b and again imagine the economy in the position represented by point z, i.e. with full employment and a deficit on the balance of payments. Now by mixing monetary contraction (raising interest rates) with fiscal expansion, the authorities may maintain the level of domestic expenditure at E_3. The raising of the interest rate, however, implies a larger net capital inflow, and consequently the maintenance of balance-of-payments equilibrium requires a lower level of the exchange rate. Graphically, this means a downward shift of the ***BB*** schedule, and a suitable policy mix will be able to shift the ***BB*** schedule until it passes through point z, in which case both internal and external balance is attained.

There are, however, several shortcomings of this analysis. Let us consider two of these, both of which focus on the short run nature of the analysis. First, according to the above analysis a once-and-for-all increase in the domestic interest rate (foreign rates remaining constant) would lead to a greater capital account surplus (or a smaller deficit) for all succeeding periods. Now it is true that such an interest rate change is likely to lead economic units to adjust their relative holdings of stocks of various assets, but, once asset stocks have adjusted sufficiently so that *actual* stocks equal *desired* stocks at the new set of relative interest rates, any tendency for further changes will disappear. In other words, wealth owners have a desired distribution of their wealth among assets in various countries, this distribution being partly dependent upon interest rate differentials. When the UK interest rate rises, so widening the differential between itself and rates in other financial centres, wealth owners will presumably shift some of their wealth towards UK assets, so causing a higher capital inflow. However, once they have made their desired portfolio adjustments such increased inflows will cease. Therefore the improvement in the balance of payments is essentially a transitory phenomenon which only occurs during the period of portfolio adjustments. It might be assumed that the world's stock of wealth is growing over time and that the allocation of this between countries depends upon interest rate differentials. In this case, a once-and-for-all increase in the UK interest rate could lead to a continuous inflow.

The second criticism of a policy that aims to induce a larger inflow of capital by raising the domestic interest rate is that no account is taken of the debt-servicing requirements that a continuous capital inflow would have on the current account of the balance of payments. Since the interest payments on the domestic economy's foreign-held assets cause the current account of the balance of payments to deteriorate (see Chapter 1), the country will be led into even fiercer applications of the policy, i.e. even higher interest rates, to attract an even greater capital inflow purely to pay interest on its past borrowings. In effect, we can say that the country will be borrowing from Peter to pay Paul (or to pay Peter?).

What are the costs to the economy of following the required monetary–fiscal policy mix? Remember that the essence of the policy is that an increase in interest rates, which will lead to a decrease in investment at home, must be accompanied either by tax reductions or by increases in government expenditure (or by some combination of the two). This raises the problem, as Johnson (1967a) notes, of 'inefficiency versus efficiency in the use of domestic saving potential'. It is argued that the monetary–fiscal policy mix technique wastes the economy's savings by channelling them into debt-financed government expenditure and away from domestic capital formation. Implicit here is the belief that government expenditure is largely unproductive and that the yield that will be needed to pay the debt financing in the future comes from future taxation, not from additional future production which the government expenditure makes possible. At the same time it is argued that the reduction in private investment expenditure leads to a fall in potential future national output.

There can, however, be no *a priori* presumption that a replacement of private investment by government investment will lead to a reduction in the growth of production potential. If the economy's growth is being held back by a lack of social capital (e.g. roads, railways, etc.) or human capital, then government expenditure may be more 'productive' than private investment. Furthermore, there may be certain divergences between social and private benefits and costs which make these expenditures more suitably undertaken by the public sector rather than the private sector.

The period 1973–4 in the United Kingdom was a time during which large current-account deficits were accompanied by large capital inflows. This period illustrates some of the problems discussed above when analysing the use of the capital account of the balance of payments for dealing with problems on the current account. The policy implied an increase in the level of domestic rates; the United Kingdom's minimum lending rate rose from $7\frac{1}{2}$ per cent in mid-1973 to 13 per cent at the end of that year. This high rate militated against domestic investment. Expenditure on fixed investment, in real terms, fell by 1 per cent during the period 1973–5. The policy is also short run in nature, not solving the basic problem and, to a certain extent, exacerbating the problem by building up a stream of future debt and redemption payments. Since the bulk of the borrowing during this period was at high commercial rates, this difficulty began to manifest itself as early as 1975. The balance on the invisible account, which includes interest payments, worsened by £130 m. during the period 1974–5; this was the first time that the invisible account had not improved since 1966.

RESTRICTIONS ON TRADE

A popular way of attempting to deal with balance-of-payments problems is to impose various restrictions, prohibitions, and sometimes incentives to take part in international trade. Since the various measures are numerous, we shall confine ourselves to the most common device, namely, the imposition of a tariff on imports.

A tariff is nothing more than a tax on imports. The effects of the imposition of a tariff are shown in Figure 6.6. At a *given exchange rate*, the UK demand for imports is given by schedule D_1, and, given the supply schedule of imports, S, which is represented as being perfectly elastic at price P_w, the United Kingdom will purchase quantity OQ_1 of imports and demand quantity OP_waQ_1 of dollars to pay for them. Now suppose that the authorities impose a tariff on imports. This means that, over and above the amount paid to the foreign supplier, the UK importer will have to pay a sum to the authorities for each unit imported. The effect of the tariff will be to shift the demand schedule downwards by the amount of the tariff, i.e. to D_T. The reasoning behind this is simple. Take, for example, quantity OQ_1. Before the tariff the importer would have been willing to offer the foreign supplier a price of OP_w per unit. Now, when the tariff of P_1P_w per unit is imposed, if the importer is still to end up paying OP_w per unit, he can offer only OP_1 to the supplier. The import market will now come to equilibrium with a quantity of imports of OQ_2 and a demand for dollars of OP_wbQ_2 on the foreign exchange market. (Note that the tariff will have had the effect of raising the domestic price of the imports.)

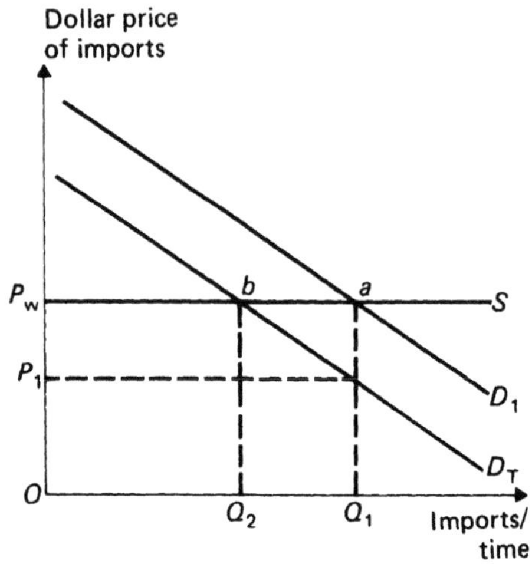

Figure 6.6 *The effect of a tariff on demand for imports*

Therefore, at the exchange rate implicit in the drawing of the schedules in Figure 6.6, the imposition of the tariff has led to a fall in the quantity of dollars demanded. The above exercise could be repeated for every other conceivable exchange rate, and the result would be that the demand schedule for foreign exchange, as shown in Figure 6.3, would shift to the left.

The fall in the demand for imports and thus for foreign exchange has important implications for the positions of the *BB* and *YY* schedules of Figure 6.4b. These effects are shown in Figure 6.7. As far as the *BB* schedule is concerned, the effect of the reduction in imports resulting from the imposition of the tariff is to shift the schedule to the right. To demonstrate this, imagine any combination of the exchange rate and the level of domestic expenditure on the *BB* schedule, i.e. a combination that gives external equilibrium. Now, with the reduction in imports resulting from the imposition of the tariff, this original combination of the exchange rate and domestic expenditure is one that yields a balance-of-payments surplus. Therefore, to regain external equilibrium at an unchanged exchange rate requires an increase in domestic expenditure, which implies a rightward shift of the *BB* schedule. This is represented in Figure 6.7 by the movement of the schedule from *BB* to B_1B_1. The effect on the *YY* schedule is to shift this to the left. Again imagine any combination on *YY*. This, as mentioned earlier, means that total demand is just sufficient to purchase the full-employment output of domestic goods and services. Therefore, at the given exchange rate a reduction in imports implies an increase in the demand for domestic output, and consequently a decrease in domestic demand is required to remove this excess demand. This

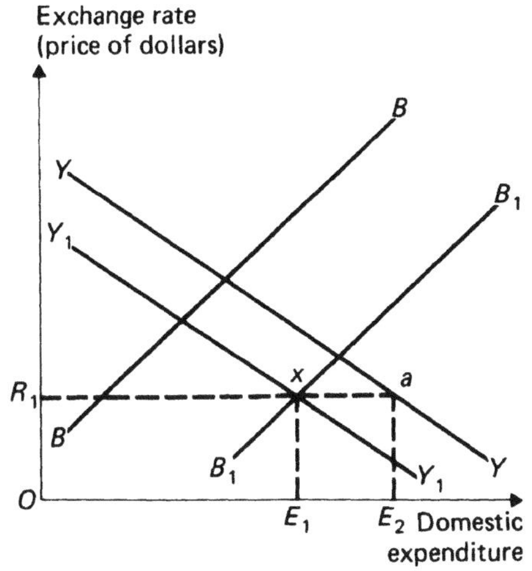

Figure 6.7 *A tariff and the achievement of internal and external equilibrium*

adjustment is represented in Figure 6.7 by the leftward shift of *YY* to $Y_1 Y_1$.

Assume that initially the economy is at position *a* in Figure 6.7, i.e. with the exchange rate at level R_1 and domestic expenditure at level E_2; there is internal balance but a balance-of-payments deficit. It should be clear, from what has been said above, that the application of a tariff alone will not attain both internal and external balance. A tariff must exist which would take schedule *BB* through point *a*. However, we now know that the tariff will also shift *YY* leftwards. This would make a position such as *a* one of excess demand for domestic output, and the resultant inflation would erode the competitive edge given to the UK import substitutes. From positions such as *a*, import restrictions can be used effectively only if the imposed tariffs make the *YY* and *BB* schedules shift until they intersect at point *x* and are accompanied by a policy of expenditure reduction from E_2 to E_1.

Therefore, as with exchange rate changes, which were mentioned in an earlier section, an 'expenditure-switching' policy will not usually be sufficient to solve the problem if the economy is close to full employment. (Both exchange rate changes and import tariffs are called 'expenditure-switching' policies, because the former, in the case of a depreciation of the domestic currency, switch foreign expenditure towards domestic exports and domestic expenditures towards import substitutes while import tariffs switch domestic expenditure also towards import substitutes.) A switching policy will usually have to be accompanied by adjustments in the level of domestic expenditure.

In November 1964 the UK authorities imposed a tariff (the

import surcharge) on imports of manufactures at a rate of 15 per cent (later reduced to 10 per cent). It has been estimated (Cooper, 1968) that the effect of this tariff was to reduce the UK import bill by £130 m. in 1965 and by £80 m. in 1966. Also, one of the policies instituted in 1968 to support the 1967 devaluation was an import deposit scheme whereby importers had to deposit 50 per cent of the value of imported manufactured goods with the government for six months. As no interest was paid on such deposits they constituted a small tariff.

Our concern is with the use of tariffs to reduce imports in order to improve a country's balance-of-payments position. However, there are many other implications of the imposition of tariffs and many criteria against which they should be judged. For a discussion of the effects of tariffs, see Scammell (1974).

POLICY ACTIONS IN THE REST OF THE WORLD

From time to time we have pointed out that changes in foreign income levels will have an impact on the United Kingdom's balance-of-payments position, e.g. by affecting the demand for exports, and during our discussion on capital flows we emphasised that it is the differential between domestic and foreign interest rates that induces capital flows. Nevertheless, much of our examination of balance-of-payments policies in this chapter has been carried out under the assumption that conditions in the rest of the world have remained unchanged. The relaxation of this assumption has important implications for the balance-of-payments policies with which we have been dealing, and it will be worthwhile to point out a few of them.

The first point to bear in mind is that any UK policy action on the balance of payments may be wholly or partly nullified by the actions of other countries. For example, an important factor in determining the effectiveness of, say, a tariff or an exchange rate change in improving a balance-of-payments position is the reaction of other countries to that policy change. After all, a reduction in the imports of one country has its counterpart in a reduction in the exports (and levels of employment) of other countries. The UK introduction in 1964 of the import surcharge was greeted with some disquiet by the other members of the European Free Trade Association (EFTA), and their complaints played a major role in bringing about the elimination of the tariff in 1966. However, if other countries react to the introduction of a tariff by, for example, instituting policies to encourage their exports and reduce their imports, the final outcome may be no improvement in the initial country's balance-of-payments position. A classic example of foreign reactions rendering unilateral policies ineffective is given by the experience of many Western economies during the depression years of the 1930s. Countries in severe depression attempted to 'export their unemployment' by discouraging imports and encouraging exports through exchange rate depreciation, the introduction of import tariffs and quotas, and export subsidies. Each country's action, however, merely tended to cancel out the deleterious effects of similar actions by other countries, with little benefit to anyone; the main effect was to bring about a sharp reduction in the volume of world trade.

A second implication of dropping the assumption of constant conditions in the rest of the world is that UK payments situations may be improved without any active policy on the part of the UK authorities, if, for example, through diplomatic action foreign authorities can be persuaded either to expand their economies (and hopefully, therefore, to increase the demand for UK exports) or to reduce their exports to the United Kingdom. Recently, the United Kingdom made such an approach to Japanese manufacturers of cars and electronic equipment.

Chapter 7

The Theory of Policy

One of the concerns of the introductory chapter was to explain what is meant by macroeconomic policy. There it was stated that it is useful to think of policy in terms of target and instrumental variables. The authorities are to be thought of as having certain desired levels for the target variables and as having under their control certain instruments that affect these targets. Policy making is then to be thought of as the manipulation of the latter in order to achieve the former. A large part of the present book has been specifically concerned with a close examination of the workings of the instrumental variables used by the authorities. The process of using the various instruments of policy to achieve simultaneously the desired levels of the target variables involves a number of conceptual and practical difficulties. In this final chapter we set out to examine some of these difficulties.

We begin with an examination of Tinbergen's 'fixed targets' approach to economic policy, which is concerned with the basic requirements for the simultaneous achievement of the desired levels of the target variables. We then consider another approach to policy – one associated with another Dutch economist, Henri Theil. Theil's approach is concerned with the situation in which all of the desired levels of the target variables cannot be achieved simultaneously and in which choices have therefore to be made. Our attention then turns to some of the practical difficulties that arise in the conduct of policy, and finally we consider briefly some views on the overall conduct of postwar macroeconomic policy in the United Kingdom.

TINBERGEN'S 'FIXED TARGETS' APPROACH

Tinbergen's approach views economic policy in terms of the dichotomy between targets and instruments. Fixed values are chosen for the target variables, and the instruments are varied in order to attain the predetermined targets. For example, the policy maker will not merely be instructed to 'reduce the rate of inflation'; instead he will be issued with more specific instructions and told to reduce the rate of inflation to, say, x per cent. The fixed targets

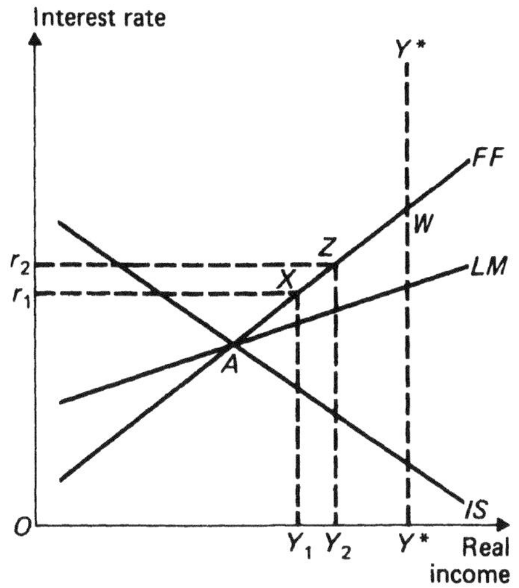

Figure 7.1 *Tinbergen's approach to policy – a two instruments–two targets example*

approach is appealing since it provides a simple condition for the simultaneous attainment of the targets. This condition is often referred to as Tinbergen's Rule. It states that if there is to be a simultaneous achievement of all the targets, then it is necessary to have at least the same number of independent effective instruments as there are independent targets. We shall illustrate the major points of this rather concise statement of Tinbergen's work using the example of an economic problem that has long interested economists. This is the problem of achieving both the targets of full-employment income and of equilibrium on the balance of payments under a regime in which exchange rates are not free to vary.

In Figure 7.1 we present a diagrammatic framework for considering problems involving an open economy, i.e. an economy in which external economic relations are explicitly taken into account. The *IS–LM* schedules (the Hicks–Hansen analysis) have already been much explored in economics (but the reader who wishes to remind himself of their meaning should see Laidler, 1969). Let it suffice here to say that the *LM* schedule shows combinations of the rate of interest and the level of real income that equate the demand and supply of money, i.e. combinations that give equilibrium in the money market, and that the *IS* schedule traces combinations of the same two variables that give equilibrium in the market for goods and services.

The *FF* schedule may be less familiar. This plots combinations of the interest rate and the level of real income that equate the balance-of-trade deficit (surplus) and the capital account surplus (deficit);

that is, balance-of-payments equilibrium is obtained along *FF*. If certain reasonably intuitive assumptions are accepted, it can be shown that this schedule will be positively sloped. These assumptions are as follows: exports are exogenous, imports depend directly on the level of domestic real income, and the surplus (deficit) on capital account will be larger (smaller) the higher is the domestic interest rate relative to interest rates ruling in other financial centres. If these other rates are assumed to be constant we can restrict our attention to the absolute level of the domestic rate. These assumptions were also used in dealing with balance-of-payments policy in Chapter 6.

Using these assumptions it is now clear that the *FF* curve must be upward sloping. Starting initially from point *X* on *FF*, an increase in real income (say from Y_1 to Y_2) must worsen the trade account, which must be offset by an increase in the interest rate (say from r_1 to r_2). The rise in the interest rate brings about an improvement in the capital account, which offsets the deterioration in the trade account. Therefore points below and to the right of *FF* represent situations of balance-of-payments deficit, whereas points above and to the left are situations of surplus. The main factor determining the precise slope of the *FF* schedule is the responsiveness of capital movements to changes in the rate of interest relative to the responsiveness of the trade balance to changes in the level of real income. The more sensitive is the capital account position to changes in the interest rate relative to the sensitivity of the trade balance to changes in real income, the less steeply sloped will be the *FF* schedule.

As the schedules are drawn in Figure 7.1, the *FF* schedule is more steeply sloped than the *LM* schedule, and this is the only case that we shall consider. However, it is possible that the *FF* schedule will be less steeply sloped than the *LM* schedule. This will be the case if capital movements are so sensitive to changes in the interest rate that the capital account of the balance of payments is improved to a greater extent, due to the increased interest rate, then the trade account deteriorates, due to the increase in real income, as a result of, say, an expansion in government expenditure.

Equality of targets and instruments

Using the framework outlined above, we shall examine some of the important aspects of the fixed targets approach. Suppose that the policy maker has been commissioned to make use of his control over monetary and fiscal policy to achieve a full-employment level of real income and equilibrium on the balance of payments. The full-employment target is given as Y^* in Figure 7.1, and since on the same diagram balance-of-payments equilibrium is obtained along *FF*, both targets will be attained at point *W*. Assuming an initial position of the economy at point *A*, the problem posed to the policy maker is to decide what he must do to achieve his income objective while maintaining balance-of-payments equilibrium, i.e. to move from point *A* to point *W*.

As we have already seen, Tinbergen's Rule states that, for a solution to the problem, the policy maker needs at least an equal number of instruments and targets. The two instruments over which we shall assume that the policy maker has control are fiscal and monetary policy. We shall represent the former by variations in government spending and the latter by changes in the money supply. Changes in government expenditure have their main effect in shifting the *IS* schedule, whereas changes in the money supply shift the *LM* schedule. The solution to the problem posed above then involves both an expansionary fiscal policy and a contractionary monetary policy, so that we obtain an intersection of the *IS* and *LM* schedules at point *W*.

Straightforward as the above framework may be, it will be useful to translate the information in Figure 7.1 into a form in which we can see more clearly the various combinations of the instrumental variables that satisfy our two targets, namely the full-employment level of income and equilibrium on the balance of payments. This is done in Figure 7.2, where schedules *YY* and *BB* respectively trace those combinations of government spending and the money supply which yield internal and external equilibrium.

The *YY* curve is obtained by shifting the intersection of the *IS* and *LM* curves, via changes in government spending and the money supply, along the vertical line Y^*Y^* in Figure 7.1. Its negative slope reflects the fact that an increase in the money supply must be accompanied by a fall in government expenditure if the *IS* and *LM* curves are to continue to intersect at income level Y^* in Figure 7.1. Points lying above and to the right of *YY* represent situations of inflationary pressure ($Y > 0$), since increasing either the money supply or the level of government expenditure from any original point on *YY* generates demand in excess of that required to maintain full-employment income. Similar reasoning tells us that points below *YY* depict situations of unemployment ($Y < 0$).

The *BB* schedule is obtained in much the same way. It shows combinations of money supply and government spending that give balance-of-payments equilibrium. It is obtained by shifting the intersection of the *IS* and *LM* curves along the *FF* curve in Figure 7.1. In Figure 7.2, points above and to the right of *BB* involve situations of balance-of-payments deficit ($B < 0$), and those below and to the left represent a balance-of-payments surplus ($B > 0$).

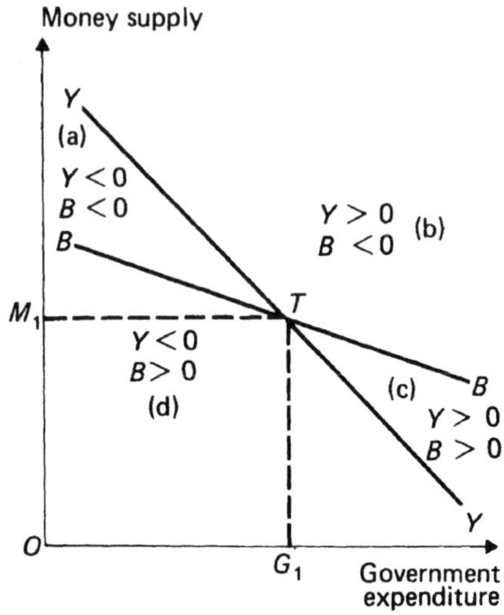

Figure 7.2 *The combination of the money supply and government expenditure that yields internal and external equilibrium*

Since both schedules are downward sloping, some explanation is due as to which has the steeper slope. *BB* is the less steeply sloped, because successive movements along *YY* will not alter the trade account of the balance of payments. However, the changes that take place in the money supply and in government expenditure, required to keep the economy on *YY*, have associated with them changes in the interest rate. These interest rate changes affect the capital account of the balance of payments. Hence starting from point *T*, where the two curves intersect, imagine a movement upwards along the *YY* curve. This involves an expansion of the money supply and a reduction in government spending, which bring about a fall in the interest rate, putting the economy into a situation of overall balance-of-payments deficit, i.e. above *BB*. A similar argument shows that to the right of point *T*, schedule *BB* will lie above schedule *YY*. The four quadrants into which Figure 7.2 is now divided represent different situations of disequilibrium: (a) involves unemployment and a payments deficit, (b) inflationary tendencies and a payments deficit, (c) inflationary tendencies and a payments surplus, and (d) unemployment and a payments surplus.

Returning to the original problem, Figure 7.2 demonstrates that there is a unique combination of the level of government expenditure and the level of money supply that results in the attainment of both targets. This is shown at government expenditure G_1 and money supply M_1. The general rule mentioned above that the number of targets and instruments should be equal tends to be supported. However, the question must be asked: what happens if the quantitative requirement does not hold? In other words, how will an excess of targets over instruments or an excess of instruments over targets affect the result? It is to these questions that our attention must now turn.

First let us consider the case in which the number of instruments exceeds the number of targets. We shall illustrate this by dropping one of the targets while retaining both instruments. If the full-employment level of income is dropped from our list of targets, this allows us to erase the *YY* curve in Figure 7.2. In this case there is an infinite number of combinations of government expenditure and money supply levels that yield the target to be achieved, namely, balance-of-payments equilibrium. Therefore we see that when the number of instruments exceeds the number of targets, the problem is that policy making necessarily involves an element of indeterminateness in that there is more than one way of combining the instruments to achieve the targets.

Turning now to the case in which the number of targets exceeds the number of effective instruments available, we illustrate the dilemma that this poses the policy maker with the aid of a simple example. Suppose that government expenditure is frozen at some arbitrary level; the policy maker is then left with only changes in the money supply to attain both of the targets. As Figure 7.2 shows, only in the highly unlikely case that government expenditure is set at G_1 can a manipulation of the money supply achieve both targets. More often than not both targets will not be achieved.

Our original statement of Tinbergen's Rule emphasised that the requirement of at least equality between targets and instruments is a necessary condition for a solution to the policy problem. Also mentioned was that the targets and instruments should be independent and that the instruments should be effective. That instruments should be effective when they are applied to target variables is intuitively obvious. While a tax on peanuts could be regarded as an instrument, it is unlikely that it would make much impression on the level of aggregate demand or on the balance of payments, even if it were applied at very high rates. We now turn to the problem of independence of targets and instruments.

The independence of instruments and of targets

Finally, the last consideration of major importance is that, in order to ensure the achievement of a solution to the policy problem, we require independence between targets and between instruments. What is the relevance of independence to the policy problem? Let us first consider the independence of instruments.

The two instruments are not independent if, for example, a

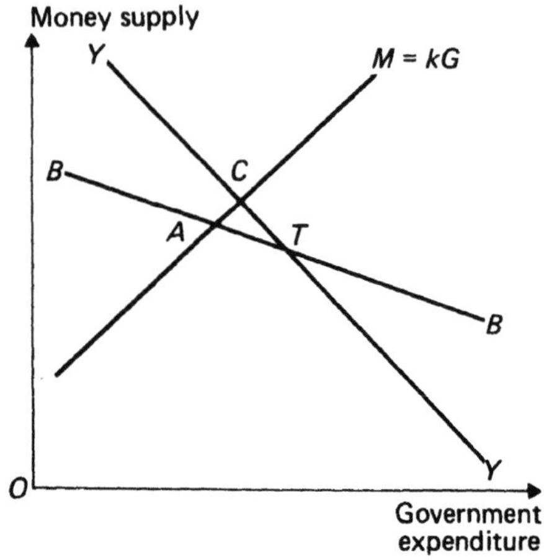

Figure 7.3 *The effect of dependence between the two instruments on the simultaneous achievement of the targets*

particular level of government expenditure implies a particular level of the money supply. For the purpose of attempting to conduct the kind of policy in which we are interested, the two instruments have effectively been collapsed into one. An illustration of the point is given in Figure 7.3, where the dependence between the two instruments is plotted as the function $M = kG$ and the schedules YY and BB are defined as above. Parameter k defines the exact functional relationship between the money supply and government expenditure. This dependence between instruments greatly limits the policy maker's scope for manoeuvre. Function $M = kG$ will pass through point T only fortuitously. In the more general case, in which it does not pass through this point, we see that both targets cannot be achieved simultaneously. The policy maker could choose levels of the instruments in order to situate at point A, satisfying the balance-of-payments target, or at point C, achieving the income target, but both targets cannot be satisfied at the same time.

So far the case of dependence between instruments has been explained. Less straightforward, however, is the situation involving dependence between targets. This occurs if the relative effectiveness of the two instruments on each of the two targets is the same. This situation is illustrated in Figure 7.4, in which the slope of the YY curve is the same as that of the BB curve. Consider an initial combination of the levels of the instrumental variables as being M_1 and G_2, which give a position of balance-of-payments equilibrium. If the money supply is increased to M_2, then in order to maintain balance-of-payments equilibrium government spending must be

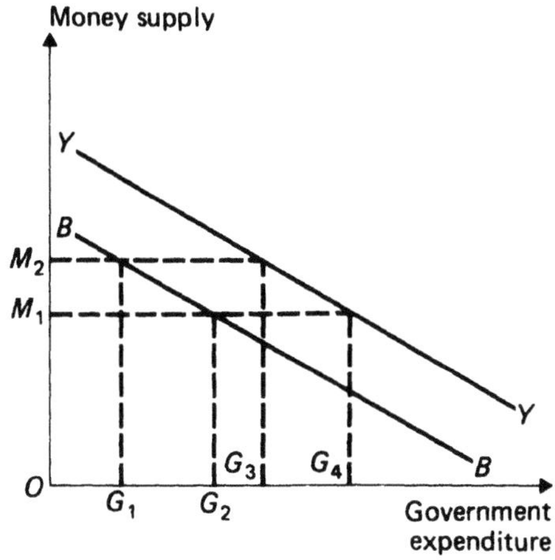

Figure 7.4 *Dependence between targets*

reduced to G_1. A measure of the relative effectiveness of the two instruments on this particular target is given by the ratio

$$-\frac{OG_2 - OG_1}{OM_2 - OM_1}$$

If the supply of money were to become a more effective instrument for operating upon the balance of payments, the slope of *BB* would become less steep. Alternatively, consider the levels of the instruments as being M_1 and G_4, which give full-employment income. Again an increase in the money supply from M_1 to M_2 must be compensated for by a reduction in the level of government spending, from G_4 to G_3, if the target level of income is to be maintained. In this case the relative effectiveness of the two instruments on the income target is given by

$$-\frac{OG_4 - OG_3}{OM_2 - OM_1}$$

The value of this ratio is equal to the previous one.

An economic explanation of the above situation would be that capital flows are totally insensitive to changes in the rate of interest. If this is so, then fiscal and monetary policies affect the balance of payments in exactly the same way, namely, via a change in the trade balance that is in both cases equal to the resulting change in income multiplied by the effect of the change in income on the trade balance. Referring back to Figure 7.1, if capital flows are totally insensitive to interest rate changes, the *FF* schedule will be a vertical line at some income level, indicating that the level of the interest rate has no impact whatever on the balance-of-payments position; the only way in which the external position is changed is by a change in the level of real income, which affects the trade account. This indicates that there is only one level of income that can accommodate balance-of-payments equilibrium, and we have no reason to suppose that that particular income level will be the full-employment level. If this were the case, however, the *FF* schedule would coincide with the vertical line Y^*Y^* in Figure 7.1 and the *BB* curve would coincide with the *YY* curve in Figure 7.4. In this strange case the two targets would have effectively collapsed into one. In the more general case, i.e. the one in which the level of income corresponding to balance-of-payments equilibrium is not the full-employment level, the two schedules will be as they are depicted in Figure 7.4. Consequently, with the use of only monetary and fiscal policy the two targets cannot be attained simultaneously. Once we assume the interest rate sensitivity of capital movements, however, as we have done previously, the slope of *BB* becomes less steep and the likelihood of a unique solution is reintroduced.

ADVANTAGES AND DISADVANTAGES OF THE FIXED TARGETS APPROACH

Theil (1956), while commenting upon Tinbergen's approach, explains that the postwar situation within which economic policy in the Netherlands had to operate was one in which 'it was only too easy for politicians to formulate inconsistent desires'. In such a situation 'Tinbergen's principle idea was that a clear insight should be given as to this problem of inconsistency'. In light of this the fixed targets approach has a great advantage in its simplicity. The economist has not only to develop a consistent policy but also to persuade politicians to accept it. This persuasion is more likely to occur the simpler is the message, and Tinbergen's formula, involving as it does equality of independent targets and instruments, is capable of being explained to people who have limited knowledge of economic theory.

The development of the approach has encouraged the belief that the authorities should have explicit policy goals rather than accept whatever values the variables in the economic system happen to take. The growth of this attitude was partly due to the disappointing performances of many Western economies in the interwar years. Now, while governments may realise that something is awry with the economy, they require a framework within which to institute consistent policies. The pragmatism of the New Deal will not work every time, and without theoretical and empirical justification such experiments are just as likely to go wrong as right. The fixed targets approach provides such a framework and is simple to explain to the politicians.

Since the message of Tinbergen's Rule is equality between instruments and targets, the approach has encouraged the healthy tendency of searching for new instruments. The more frequent use of prices and incomes policies since 1945, and the recent willingness to make more frequent use of the exchange rate (see Chapter 6) as an instrument (rather than an objective) of policy, are indications of this tendency.

Another of the advantages of the fixed targets approach is the importance that it places on precise quantitative information about the structural parameters of the economic system. The essence of the approach is to use knowledge of the linkages between instrumental and target variables so that the instrumental variables can be manipulated in order to achieve simultaneously the desired levels of the target variables. However, knowledge of the linkages between instrumental and target variables can only be obtained by increased use of econometric techniques. The careful estimation of the structural relations in the economy is a necessary prerequisite for the application of the fixed targets approach, and this can do nothing but help to eradicate the mistakes attributable to qualitative economic policy.

The drawbacks of the fixed targets approach have been divided by Fleming (1968) into two categories, namely, those which are essentially misapplications of the approach and those which are inherent in the approach itself. The misapplication has been caused by the fact that the 'fixed target economist' has tended to regard the selection of targets as being outside his field of interest, seeing his function merely as finding the necessary number of instruments to attain the targets. This tendency for the economist to stay aloof from the area of target formulation has led to variables becoming targets that have little or no welfare significance, e.g. stability in bond markets (see Chapter 4). However, this problem does not deal a fatal blow to the approach. It just suggests that the economist should come into the picture at an earlier stage, i.e. at the stage of target choice, pointing out the welfare significance, or lack of it, of the various possible targets.

More serious are the inherent weaknesses of the approach itself. To illustrate these weaknesses, let us refer to Figure 7.5. This demonstrates the inconsistency in policy formulation that would occur if we had three independent targets, namely, income, balance-of-payments equilibrium, and a 'target' level of the interest rate (for the reason of maintaining a particular rate of domestic investment in order to achieve a desired rate of economic growth). In Figure 7.5

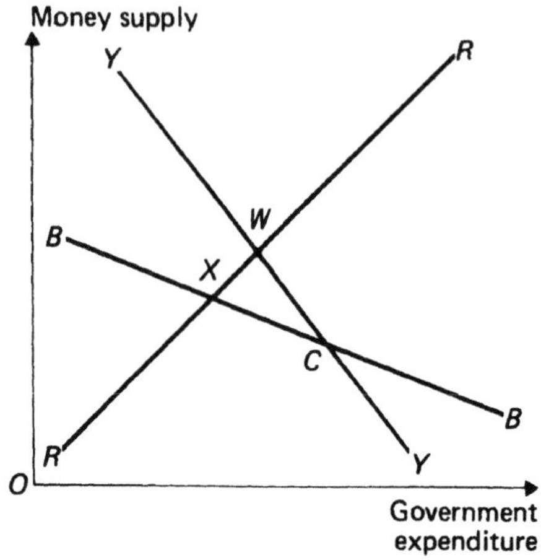

Figure 7.5 *A three targets–two instruments case*

schedule *RR* gives combinations of the money supply and government expenditure that yield a given rate of interest. It is upward sloping, which indicates that a rise in government expenditure must be accompanied by an increase in the money supply if the rate of interest is to remain unchanged. The fundamental weakness of the approach illustrated here is that it leaves open the question of what to do in a situation where any of two targets can be achieved but not all of them simultaneously. In this case some method of choice must be found. This choice implies some kind of preference or utility function that ranks the options available to the policy maker in order of preference. The preference function implied by the fixed targets approach is, as Fleming (1968) states, 'one in which each possible situation is ranked according to the number and identity of target variables having prescribed values which it contains . . . Of these situations the one with the preferred fixed targets is to be chosen.'

In terms of our example, the only situations that enter this preference function are the combinations of the targets achieved, given by point *X* where the balance-of-payments and interest rate targets are attained, point *W* where the income and interest rate targets are attained, and finally point *C* where the balance-of-payments and income targets are attained. Suppose we are told that the preference function ranks *X* as the most preferred, *W* as next best preferred and *C* as the least preferred. Then the policy maker would set the instrument levels so as to arrive at point *X*. Therefore, all situations are excluded from the preference function except the fixed (desired) target levels.

Although at point *X* two of the targets are achieved, the deviation of income from its desired level may be too substantial to be acceptable. It is conceivable that the policy maker may wish to trade off some of the attained targets against the unattained target. That is, a situation in which most of the target variables are in the neighbourhood of their desired levels (but are not actually achieved) may well be preferred to the situation in which some of the target variables are at their desired levels while others are substantially away from their desired levels. The problem then becomes not one of attaining the maximum number of most preferred targets but rather one of maximising a welfare function containing the target variables as its arguments. The advantage of this approach is that it realises that when all fixed targets cannot be attained, due to an insufficient number of effective independent instruments, the optimal policy will be to obtain the best compromise among all the targets rather than to choose the preferred combination of fixed target levels and discard the other targets.

THEIL'S FLEXIBLE TARGETS APPROACH

At the end of the last section we briefly mentioned an alternative to Tinbergen's approach. This is the so-called flexible targets approach, in which a preference function is specified which is a continuous function of the levels of the target variables. So far we have merely referred to a preference function without stating explicitly whose preferences we are considering. For simplicity we may say that we are concerned with those of the policy maker. However, if by policy maker we mean one individual who has been commissioned to formulate policy, we are in effect setting this one person up as a dictator in respect of the conduct of economic policy. In a democratic society, in which governments are elected and dismissed through the ballot box, this is hardly realistic enough. Presumably, those who are responsible for the execution of policy must reflect the wishes of their electorate, but, given this, there are important difficulties with the whole concept of amalgamating diverse individual choices into a social preference function. One particular difficulty in this field is expressed in Arrow's 'impossibility theorem'. The debate surrounding this problem is too complex for detailed discussion in a text such as this, and we refer the reader to Peston (1974) for a detailed undergraduate explanation of this controversy.

It is the nature of the flexible targets approach that there is no requirement for an equality between instruments and targets, and consequently it is not necessary to discard some of the target variables. The essence of the approach is to specify a preference function that is maximised subject to an empirical constraint. The most popular variant of Theil's work on the specification of a

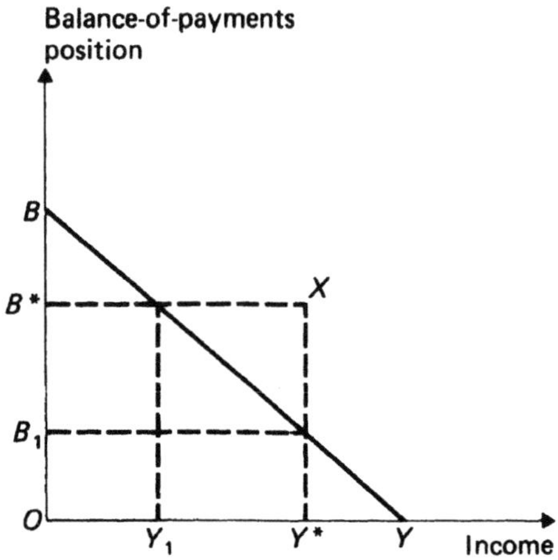

Figure 7.6 *An empirical constraint*

preference function is the *least-squares preference function*, in which utility is inversely related to a weighted sum of squares of deviations of the actual target-variable values from their desired levels. The object of the policy maker is to attain the situation where this weighted sum of squares is minimised subject to the empirical constraint.

This statement of the flexible targets approach is somewhat concise and requires elaboration. In order to explain these concepts more fully, let us consider a typical problem with which the approach is meant to deal, i.e. one in which there are more targets than effective instruments. Again we use two targets, namely, income and balance of payments. However, now we shall imagine that the only instrument at the disposal of the policy maker is that of government expenditure.

The problem is illustrated in Figure 7.6. The level of national income is measured along the horizontal axis whereas the balance-of-payments position is measured up the vertical axis. Moving up the vertical axis represents an improvement in the balance of payments. Let Y^* and B^* represent the desired national income level and desired balance-of-payments position respectively. Therefore, point X represents the simultaneous achievement of the desired levels of the target variables. However, given our assumption that only one instrument, namely, government expenditure, is available to the policy maker, line BY indicates the best possible combinations of income levels and balance-of-payments positions that can be achieved. For example, if the instrument is used to achieve the target national income level, Y^*, then the best balance-of-payments position that can be achieved is B_1. Similarly, if the target balance-of-payments position, B^*, is achieved, this implies a maximum

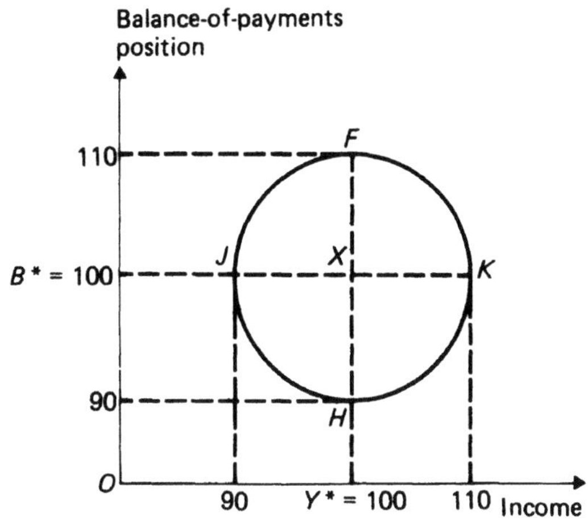

Figure 7.7 *An indifference curve when weights are equal*

income level of Y_1. Line BY is the constraint under which the policy maker must operate. He cannot achieve combinations above and to the right of BY; that is, under the given conditions, the achievement of X is not possible.

This empirical constraint then lets the policy maker know what he can have. As already mentioned, a decision as to which combination is the optimum one involves the specification of a preference function, and it was one of Theil's contributions to specify the nature of such a function. Given the desired levels for the balance of payments and income as B^* and Y^* respectively, i.e. the combination X in Figure 7.6, a representation of Theil's suggested function is

$$U = -[w_1(Y - Y^*)^2 + w_2(B - B^*)^2]$$

That is, utility is the negative of a weighted sum of squares of deviations of the actual target variable values, Y and B, from their desired values, Y^* and B^*, where w_1 and w_2 are the weights. What will the indifference curves generated by such a function look like?

Assume that weights w_1 and w_2 are initially set equal to each other at unity and that the desired levels of balance of payments, B, and income, Y, are both 100; that is, $B^* = 100$ and $Y^* = 100$. Figure 7.7 illustrates the situation. Point X represents the case in which the two desired target levels are met. At point X, welfare is at a maximum. If we allow income to remain at its desired level of 100 and the balance of payments to take the value of either 90 or 110, it should be clear that, given the utility function specified above, the policy maker is indifferent between points F and H. Similarly, if the balance of payments remains at $B^* = 100$ and we

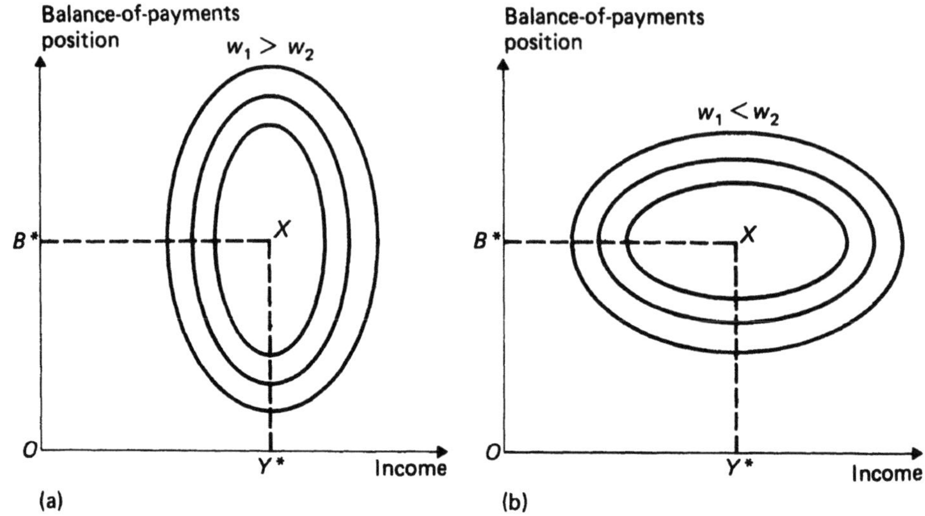

Figure 7.8 *Indifference curves when weights are unequal*

consider points *J* and *K*, the policy maker is indifferent between *J* and *K*. Since the weights are equal, by assumption, the points *F*, *K*, *H* and *J* represent the same level of utility. This can be generalised to give one indifference curve passing through these four points. Such an indifference curve represents combinations of levels of the balance-of-payments position and of income that yield the same level of utility. For other utility levels we can imagine other circular indifference curves, resulting in an indifference map which comprises concentric circles centred on point *X*. If the notion is introduced that the weights are no longer equal, i.e. that the policy maker may be prepared to accept, say, larger deviations from his desired income target than from his desired balance-of-payments target, then the indifference curves are no longer represented by circles. Depending upon which target he 'favours' most, the preference function will be represented by a set of ellipses, centred upon point *X*. Figure 7.8a depicts the indifference curves if $w_1 > w_2$, i.e. if the policy maker is less happy about deviations from Y^* than about those from B^*, and Figure 7.8b represents the opposite situation. The reader should note that the indifference curves successively further away from point *X* represent levels of lower and lower utility.

The task of the policy maker is to minimise this disutility, given the constraint under which he is forced to operate. Bringing the empirical constraint of Figure 7.6 into relation with the kind of preference function just outlined gives Figure 7.9. As this is drawn, the desired combination of balance-of-payments position and income is not attainable, since point *X* lies outside the empirical

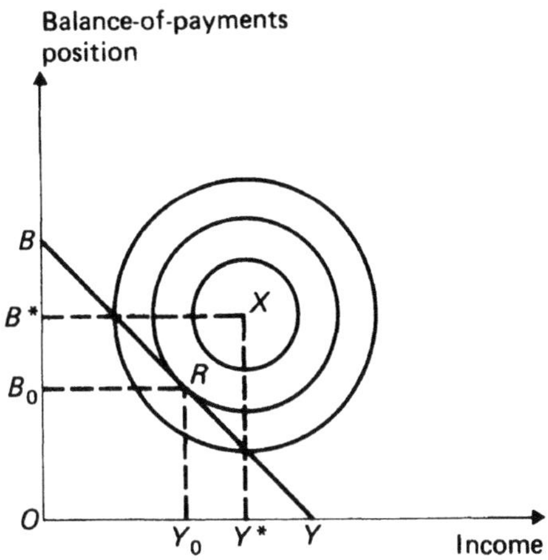

Figure 7.9 *Choice of optimum target values*

possibilities. The optimum solution is found at point *R*, giving income level Y_0 and balance-of-payments position B_0, where the constraint *BY* is tangential to a circular indifference curve. Given the circumstances, this is the best that the policy maker can achieve.

DYNAMIC PROBLEMS AND ECONOMIC FORECASTING

In the earlier sections of this chapter we illustrated the fixed targets approach to the simultaneous achievement of the desired levels of a given number of target variables with the use of a simplified two-target and two-instrument example. Although this simplification was justified for reasons of exposition, in the real world the picture is more complex.

Our outline of the approach above was under the assumption that the policy maker knew what the current levels of the variables were and that the target variables change instantaneously in response to the changes in the instrumental variables. In the real world, however, economic policy is conducted in a dynamic context, and this greatly complicates attempts at achieving the desired levels of the target variables. The policy maker does not have knowledge of the current state of the economy. Information on the actual level of unemployment, the level of industrial output, the balance-of-payments position, and so on is only known by him after some time as statistics are gathered and processed. Furthermore, if a decision is taken to alter the level of one or more of the instrumental variables in an attempt to 'push' the target variables towards their desired levels, the target variables do not respond instantaneously; more time is required before the policy change has full effect. Consequently, because of the existence of lags in the economic system, the policy change may have its effect some time after the situation for which it was originally intended. If, in the meantime, other changes have occurred which have affected the levels of the target variables, the policy change may have a perverse effect. That is, the policy change may actually have the effect of moving the levels of the target variables away from the desired levels. One criticism of UK policy throughout much of the postwar period was that the use of fiscal policy in an attempt to stabilise the level of economic activity had just this effect, i.e. that the policy turned out to be destabilising instead of stabilising. However, in Chapter 2 we saw that, because of certain difficulties in attempting to assess this contention, no firm conclusion can be reached.

The realisation of the problems that arise due to inadequate information about the current state of the economy has resulted in increased efforts, on the part of the government and other interested bodies, e.g. the National Institute of Economic and Social Research (NIESR), to make forecasts of the movements of the main economic variables. The aim of such forecasts is to aid policy making in that, if the authorities 'know' what course, say, national income will take over the next eighteen months, they can undertake policy changes now in an effort to alter that course to their desired one.

The basis of economic forecasting is the construction of a model of the economy that attempts to indicate the interdependencies of the variables of the economic system. Today such models tend to be rather sophisticated affairs dealing with the relationships between hundreds of variables. However, the variables of an economic model may be usefully classified into three groups: endogenous variables, exogenous variables that are not under the authorities' control, and exogenous variables that are under the authorities' control, namely, instrumental variables. Endogenous variables (which include the target variables) are those whose levels are determined within the model. Exogenous variables of the first type listed above are those whose levels are determined outside the model, e.g. exports. Instrumental variables, which are also exogenous variables in that their levels are determined outside the model, are represented by, for example, government expenditure and tax rates. (Note that tax rates are instrumental variables whereas the total of tax revenues is not, since this varies with the level of national income and is therefore determined within the economic system. See Chapter 2.)

Economic forecasts are usually made under the assumption that there is to be no change in existing policies, i.e. no change in the planned levels of the instrumental variables. Given the values that the instrumental variables are to take, the forecaster also needs to know what the values of the exogenous variables that are not under his control, e.g. exports, will be in the future. A forecast of the future trend in exports, for example, may be obtained on the basis of expected trends in world trade.

Using the economic model and a knowledge of the values of the instrumental variables and the other exogenous variables allows a forecast to be made of the course of the endogenous variables (which include the target variables). Such forecasts provide a basis for policy in that, if the forecast indicates a divergence between the projected course and the desired course of a target variable, policy changes can be made in an attempt to correct for this.

Stated in this way, economic forecasting appears to be straightforward. However, this is not the case; forecasting has many associated difficulties. The first difficulty involves the construction of the economic model upon which the forecasts are based. An economic model is a theoretical construct and as such is unlikely to be a complete picture of the workings of the economic system. Furthermore, the quantitative relationships between the variables in the model will have been obtained by 'fitting' the model to past data, and this will have been done with a degree of inaccuracy.

There are certain factors that will have an influence on future values of the variables in the economic system but which are difficult (or impossible?) to incorporate into a formal model. As an example we can mention the effect of changes in the 'level of confidence' of businessmen on industrial investment. Similarly, what formal economic model could have allowed for the raising of fuel prices following the Middle East war in 1973? Such difficulties can obviously lead to inaccurate forecasts and therefore to inappropriate policy responses.

CONCLUSION

It is generally agreed between economists that UK economic management in the postwar period cannot be regarded as having been totally successful. However, views differ on the reason for the lack of success. Worswick (1977) sees one reason for the lack of success, not in that the government has been unable to 'control' the economy as such, but in that during the postwar period there has been an insufficiency of effective instruments to achieve simultaneously the objectives of macroeconomic policy.

Throughout much of the postwar period the major instrument of macroeconomic policy was 'general demand management', the main aspects of which were frequent changes in rates of taxation backed up by alterations in the conditions of hire purchase and in direct controls on bank lending. Demand was expanded by the use of these techniques when it was considered desirable to raise the level of employment and the rate of growth of output, and it was contracted usually at times of balance-of-payments crises in order to support the exchange rate. However, by itself this 'steering' of the economy by general demand management could not have been expected to achieve simultaneously all the objectives of policy. Other instruments of policy were used from time to time, e.g. prices and incomes policies and exchange rate changes. However, Worswick argues that UK knowledge of the workings of these additional instruments leaves much to be desired and that more work needs to be done to estimate their effects more precisely. In the case of prices and incomes, the United Kingdom still has yet to institute a policy that will be widely accepted and workable. Worswick's conclusion is therefore that 'if the limited role of demand management in securing full employment is recognised, and it is buttressed by other instruments of policy, above all incomes policy, one can envisage the return to low unemployment and low inflation'.

On the other hand, there are those who are less optimistic than Worswick about the ability of the government to 'fine tune' the economy, because of the likelihood of the government's discretionary action creating instability due to the existence of lags in the response of target variables to policy changes. Consequently, some economists in this group, e.g. the so-called monetarists, are led to propose some simple rule, which in the case of the monetarists is to allow an expansion of the supply of money that is commensurate with the real growth potential of the economy.

References

Allen, R. and Savage, D., 'Indexing personal income taxation', in *Indexing for Inflation*, eds T. Leisner and M. A. King (London, Heinemann Educational Books, 1975).

Artis, M. J., 'Fiscal policy for stabilization', in *The Labour Government's Economic Record, 1964–70*, ed. W. Beckerman (London, Duckworth, 1972).

Artus, J., 'The 1967 devaluation of the pound sterling', *IMF Staff Papers* (November 1975).

Bank of England, 'Official transactions in the gilt-edged market', *Quarterly Bulletin* (June 1966).

Bank of England, 'The importance of money', *Quarterly Bulletin* (June 1970).

Bank of England (1971), 'Competition and credit control', *Quarterly Bulletin* (June 1971).

Bank of England (1971a), 'Key issues in monetary and credit policy', *Quarterly Bulletin* (June 1971).

Beckerman, W., *In Defence of Economic Growth* (London, Jonathan Cape, 1974).

Berstein Committee, *The Balance of Payments Statistics of the United States: A Review and Appraisal* (Washington, Government Printing Office, 1965).

Beveridge, W. H., *Full Employment in a Free Society* (London, George Allen & Unwin, 1944).

Blinder, A. S. and Solow, R., 'Analytical foundations of fiscal policy', in *The Economics of Public Finance*, A. S. Blinder *et al.* (Washington, Brookings Institution, 1974).

Bowers, J., Chesire, P., Webb, A. and Weeden, R., 'Some aspects of unemployment and the labour market, 1966–71', *National Institute Economic Review* (November 1972).

Bristow, J. A., 'Taxation and income stabilisation', *Economic Journal* (March 1968).

Bronfenbrenner, M. and Holzman, F. D., 'A survey of inflation theory', in *Surveys of Economic Theory*, Vol. I (London, Royal Economic Society/American Economic Association, Macmillan, 1965).

Canadian Royal Commission on Taxation (Ottawa, Queen's Printer, 1966).

Cooper, R. N., 'Balance of payments in review', *Journal of Political Economy* (August 1966).

Cooper, R. N., 'The balance of payments', in *Britain's Economic Prospects*, R. E. Caves *et al.* (London, George Allen & Unwin, 1968).

Cmnd 6527, *White Paper on Employment Policy* (London, HMSO, 1944).

Cmnd 9725, *White Paper on the Economic Implications of Full Employment* (London, HMSO, 1956).

Cmnd 2639, *Prices and Incomes Policy* (London, HMSO, 1965).

Department of Employment, *Prices and Earnings in 1951–69* (London, HMSO, 1971).

Fleming, J. M., 'Targets and instruments', *IMF Staff Papers* (August 1968).

Flemming, J. S., 'Trends in company profitability', *Bank of England Quarterly Bulletin* (March 1976).

Friedman, M., 'The role of monetary policy', *American Economic Review* (March 1968).

Gujarati, D., 'The behaviour of unemployment and unfilled vacancies', *Economic Journal* (March 1972).

Hansen, B., *Fiscal Policy in Seven Countries, 1955–65* (Paris, OECD, 1969).

Hansen, B., 'Excess demand, unemployment, vacancies and wages', *Quarterly Journal of Economics* (February 1970).

Harberler, G., *Inflation and the Unions* (London, Institute of Economic Affairs, 1972).

Harrod, R., 'The issues: five views', in *Inflation as a Global Problem*, ed. R. Hinshaw (Baltimore, Johns Hopkins Press, 1972).

Heller, W. W., *New Dimensions in Political Economy* (New York, W. W. Norton, 1966).

Hines, A. G., 'Trade unions and wage inflation in the UK, 1893–1961', *Review of Economic Studies* (October 1964).

Houthakker, H. and Magee, S., 'Income and price elasticities in world trade', *Review of Economics and Statistics* (May 1969).

Johnson, H. G. (1967), *Essays in Monetary Economics* (London, George Allen & Unwin, 1967).

Johnson, H. G. (1967a), 'Theoretical problems of the international monetary system', *Pakistan Development Review*, vol. 7 (1967).

Johnson, H. G., *Inflation and the Monetarist Controversy* (Amsterdam, North Holland Publishing Co., 1972).

Kaldor, N., 'Conflicts in national economic objectives', in *Conflicts in Policy Objectives*, ed. N. Kaldor (London, Blackwell, 1971).

Laidler, D. E. W., *The Demand for Money* (Scranton, Penn., International Textbook Co., 1969).

Laidler, D. E. W., 'The Phillips curve, expectations and incomes policy', in *The Current Inflation*, eds H. G. Johnson and A. R. Nobay (London, Macmillan, 1971).

Lipsey, R. G. and Parkin, J. M., 'Incomes policy: a re-appraisal', *Economica* (May 1970).

Lipsey, R. G., 'The micro theory of the Phillips curve reconsidered: a reply to Holmes and Smyth', *Economica* (February 1974).

Machlup, F., 'Three concepts of the balance of payments and the so-called dollar shortage', *Economic Journal* (March 1950).

Malkiel, B. G., *The Term Structure of Interest Rates* (Morristown, NJ, General Learning Press, 1973).

Matthews, R. C. O., 'The role of demand management', in *Britain's Economic Prospects Reconsidered*, ed. Sir A. Cairncross (London, George Allen & Unwin, 1971).

Meiselman, D., 'Role of money in national economic policy', in *Controlling Monetary Aggregates* (Federal Reserve Bank of Boston, 1969).

Metcalfe, J. S., 'Foreign trade and the balance of payments', in *The UK Economy: A Manual of Applied Economics*, 6th edn, eds A. R. Prest and D. J. Coppock (London, Weidenfeld & Nicolson, 1976).

Miller, M. H., 'Can a rise in import prices be inflationary and deflationary?', *American Economic Review* (September 1976).

Mishan, E. J., *The Costs of Economic Growth* (Harmondsworth, Penguin Books, 1969).

Mishan, E. J., *The Economic Growth Debate: An Assessment* (London, George Allen & Unwin, 1977).

Modigliani, F. and Sutch, R., 'Innovations in interest rate policy', *American Economic Review, Papers and Proceedings* (May 1966).

Modigliani, F. and Sutch, R., 'Debt management and the term structure of interest rates: an empirical analysis', *Journal of Political Economy* (August 1967).

Monopolies Commission, *Barclay's Bank Ltd, Lloyd's Bank Ltd, and Martin's Bank Ltd: Report on the Proposed Merger* (London, HMSO, 1968).

Mundell, R. A., 'The appropriate use of monetary and fiscal policy for internal and external stability', *IMF Staff Papers* (March 1962).

Musgrave, R. A. and Miller, M. H., 'Built-in flexibility', *American Economic Review* (March 1948).

Musgrave, R. A. and Musgrave, P. B., 'Fiscal policy', in *Britain's Economic Prospects*, R. E. Caves *et al.* (London, George Allen & Unwin, 1968).
National Board for Prices and Incomes, Report No. 34, *Bank Charges*, Cmnd 3292 (London, HMSO, 1967).
National Institute of Economic and Social Research (NIESR), 'The effects of the devalutation of 1967 on the current balance of payments', *Economic Journal Supplement* (March 1972).
Paish, F., 'The limits of incomes policy', in *Policy for Incomes*, ed. J. Hennessy Hobart Paper no. 29 (London, Institute of Economic Affairs, 1968).
Parkin, J. M., Jones, R. A. and Sumner, M. T., 'A survey of the econometric evidence of the effects of incomes policies on the rate of inflation', in *Incomes Policy and Inflation*, eds J. M. Parkin and M. T. Sumner (Manchester, Manchester University Press, 1972).
Parkin, J. M., Sumner, M. T. and Ward, R., 'The effects of excess demand, generalised expectations and wage–price controls on wage inflation in the UK' (University of Manchester Inflation Workshop Discussion Paper 7402, 1974).
Pearse, P. H., 'Automatic stabilization and the British taxes on income', *Review of Economic Studies* (February 1962).
Peston, M. H., 'The micro-economics of the Phillips curve', in *The Current Inflation*, eds H. G. Johnson and A. R. Nobay (London, Macmillan, 1971).
Peston, M. H., *Theory of Macroeconomic Policy* (Deddington, Philip Allan, 1974).
Phillips, A. W., 'The relationship between unemployment and rate of change of money wage rates in the UK, 1861–1957', *Economica* (November 1958).
Poole, W., 'Optimal choice of monetary policy instruments in a simple stochastic macro model', *Quarterly Journal of Economics* (May 1970).
Prest, A. R., 'Sense and nonsense in budgetary policy', *Economic Journal* (March 1968).
Radcliffe Committee, *Report of the Working of the Monetary System*, Cmnd 827 (London, HMSO, 1959).
Ross, M. H., 'Operation Twist: a mistaken policy?', *Journal of Polical Economy* (April 1966).
Saunders, P. G. and Nobay, A. R., 'Price expectations, the Phillips curve and incomes policy', in *Incomes Policy and Inflation*, eds J. M. Parkin and M. T. Sumner (Manchester, Manchester University Press, 1972).
Scammell, W. M., *International Trade and Payments* (London, Macmillan, 1974).
Shaw, G. K., *An Introduction to the Theory of Macro-economic Policy* (London, Martin Robertson, 1971).
Smyth, D. J., 'Can "automatic stabilizers" be destabilizing?', *Public Finance*, vol. 18, no. 3–4 (1963).
Smyth, D. J., 'Built-in flexibility of taxation and automatic stabilization', *Journal of Political Economy* (August 1966).
Smyth, D. J., 'The full employment budget surplus: is it a useful guide to policy?', *Public Policy* (Winter 1970).
Smyth, D. J., 'A note on built-in flexibility of taxation and stability when tax liabilities respond with a time lag', *Economic and Social Review*, vol. 7, pt 1 (1975).
Snyder, W. W., 'Measuring economic stabilization: 1955–65', *American Economic Review* (December 1970).
Solow, R., 'Investment and technical progress', in *Mathematical Methods in the Social Sciences*, eds K. Arrow, S. Karlin and P. Suppes (Stanford, Stanford University Press, 1959).
Solow, R., *Price Expectations and the Behaviour of the Price Level* (Manchester, Manchester University Press, 1969).
Taylor, J., 'The behaviour of unemployment and unfilled vacancies: GB 1958–71: an alternative view', *Economic Journal* (December 1972).
Taylor, J., *Unemployment and Wage Inflation* (Harlow, Longman, 1974).

Theil, H., 'On the theory of economic policy', *American Economic Review, Papers and Proceedings* (May 1956).
Thirlwall, A. P. (1969), 'Types of unemployment with special reference to non demand-deficient unemployment in Great Britain', *Scottish Journal of Political Economy* (February 1969).
Thirlwall, A. P. (1969a), 'Unemployment compensation as an automatic stabiliser', *Bulletin of the Oxford University Institute of Economics and Statistics* (February 1969).
Thirlwall, A. P. (1974), 'Types of unemployment in the regions of Great Britain', *Manchester School of Economic and Social Studies* (December 1974).
Thirlwall, A. P. (1974a), 'The panacea of the floating pound', *National Westminster Bank Review* (August 1974).
Tobin, J., 'Commercial banks as creators of money', in *Banking and Monetary Studies*, ed. D. Carson (Homewood, Ill., Irwin, 1963).
Winch, D., *Economics and Policy: A Historical Survey* (London, Hodder & Stoughton, 1969).
Worswick, G. D. N., 'Fiscal policy and stabilization in Britain', in *Britain's Economic Prospects Reconsidered*, ed. Sir A. Cairncross (London, George Allen & Unwin, 1970).
Worswick, G. D. N., 'The end of demand management?' *Lloyds Bank Review* (January 1977).

Index

For Product Safety Concerns and Information please contact our EU representative GPSR@taylorandfrancis.com Taylor & Francis Verlag GmbH, Kaufingerstraße 24, 80331 München, Germany

Batch number: 10725802

Printed by Printforce, the Netherlands